Special Needs
Handbook for Teachers

Classroom Management & Learning Strategies for Success

Author: Molly Millians & The Do2Learn Team

For more information, visit www.Do2Learn.com

This handbook was supported by Grant Number R44 AA013362 from the National Institutes of Health. The content is solely the responsibility of the authors and does not necessarily represent the official views of the National Institute of Alcohol Abuse and Alcoholism or the National Institutes of Health.

Author: Molly Millians & The Do2Learn Team

ISBN: 978-1-60323-004-9 (Paperback)

This book is printed on acid free paper.

Table of Contents

Table of Contents

Table of Contents

Table of Contents

SPECIAL NEEDS Handbook for Teachers

For more than 10 years we have been providing resources and guidance for teachers of children with special needs through our web site, Do2Learn.com. While many things can affect a child's progress, over time we have gathered a collection of best practices and ideas that our millions of users have told us work with many of the children in their classrooms. This handbook, the brainstorm of Molly Millians, is designed to share these techniques with you.

Like our website, this handbook combines explanations with the print material needed to implement them. Because we know how frustrating it can be for teachers to find time to make grid paper, forms, organizers, and the many suggested helpers, the Appendix contains most referenced resources. Where the material is available free from our website, Do2Learn.com, we may show how to implement ideas but not include the forms in the Appendix. This is primarily because the site has thousands of pages of resources and including everything in this handbook would make it costly to print. Downloadable resources can be found in the do2learn site navigation bar headings '*Activities*', '*Get Organized*', and '*Picture Cards*'. '*Songs and Games*' has the "Safety Songs", "Feelings", "Facial Expressions", and "Math Mahjong" games. And as a last resort, the '*Site Map*' at Do2Learn.com lists everything.

The handbook also shows examples of some of our products that we sell at the site, such as the <u>Make-A-Schedule</u> picture card program and the Fine Motor Skills Activity Book. We have included samples from these products to help you get started, but they are too extensive to duplicate in this handbook (For example, <u>Make-A-Schedule</u> has thousands of color picture cards in several sizes as well as forms and templates).

While this book is a great combination of classroom resources for teachers of children with special needs, there are also many items and ideas available at do2learn.com and in our other products that we don't include because of space limitations. We recommend that you try all that we offer and find the combination that works best for your class.

From the Do2Learn Team

Acknowledgements

Special thanks are given to Claire Coles, PhD, Elles Taddeo, Ed.D, Julie Kable, PhD, Laurie Foudin, PhD, and Jason Lazarow for their ideas and patience and support of the program.

Part I
Classroom Management

Contents:

Chapter I
Classroom Environment

Children with special needs require a safe, nurturing environment that provides reasonable expectations and educational supports to succeed in school. They may be easily distracted in a space that contains a multitude of colors, directive and interesting posters, and elaborate displays. Extraneous hall noise, student activity, smells from the lunchroom, hums from fluorescent lighting systems, and noise from heating/air-conditioning systems and electrical or mechanical gadgets can also be distracting. Children with special needs benefit from a calm and predictable classroom setting that considers the classroom layout, seating arrangements, and access to materials.

▶▶▶ **Tips for creating a calming and predictable environment:**

- Simplify room layout by designating specific areas for defined activities. The examples below of a Pre-K classroom show distinct areas for activities such as reading, work, snack, and music. Clearly label the areas and storage using color coding or a pictorial system.

Bathroom
A table and labeled baskets help organize children's extra clothes and diapers. Picture cards that show the toileting sequence are posted above the toilet.

Toys
Toy shelves stay neat and organized by taping a photo of the toy on the shelf and then matching the image with the real thing.

Cubbies
Each child has her own space to store her book bag, lunch box, and extra clothes. The cubby is labeled with her name and photograph.

Classroom Environment

Overview

Puzzles
The puzzle racks are on top of the shelves that store fine motor skills activities. A "work" pocket is on the side of the shelf. When children enter this center, they put their name card in the pocket.

Workboxes
Colorful plastic work boxes keep materials organized and accessible. Each box is labeled with words and a picture. Examples of these activities include matching, counting, sorting, and clipping.

- Designate specific areas for quiet work.

- Only post necessary information such as schedules, examples of children's work, classroom expectations, and information that is to be used for instruction.

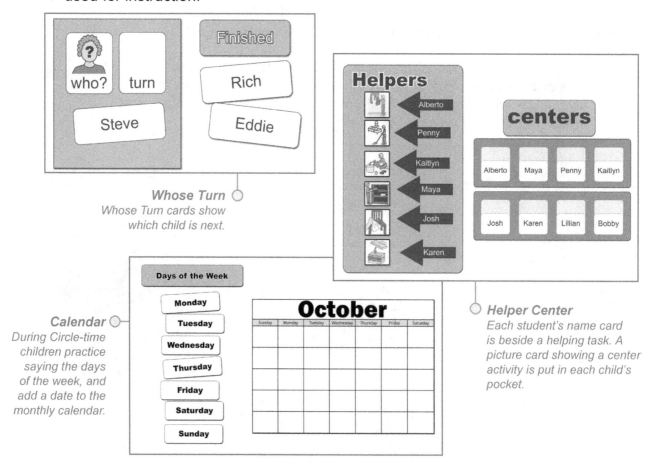

Whose Turn
Whose Turn cards show which child is next.

Calendar
During Circle-time children practice saying the days of the week, and add a date to the monthly calendar.

Helper Center
Each student's name card is beside a helping task. A picture card showing a center activity is put in each child's pocket.

▶▶▶**Careful seating arrangements can lessen distractions:**

- Seat away from doorways, windows, and high-traffic areas such as the pencil sharpener.

- Place easily distracted children and those who require the most assistance near the instructor.

- Provide special types of seating arrangement for quiet or calm down areas of the room. Examples are a "thinking time" chair that acts as a quick reminder about the consequences of inappropriate actions, where children sit away from teacher and peer reinforcement, and a "waiting chair" to help diffuse the anxiety of waiting for a turn.

Thinking & Waiting Chairs
When children need "thinking time" or a quick reminder about the consequences of inappropriate actions, they sit in the thinking chair away from teacher and peer reinforcement. Designate a special chair to help diffuse the anxiety of waiting for a turn.

Classroom Environment

Overview

- Feet support can help for short legs that cannot reach the ground.

- Floor lamps and non-fluorescent lighting systems can eliminate some of the extraneous sounds and glare. Remove fluorescent lights and replace them with string of lights that are above each desk to cut glare. Use as much natural lightening as possible.

Feet Support
Old phone directories duct taped together form a support for small feet.

- If children are easily distracted by noise, use headphones that cover the whole ears (not earplugs) to block out sounds. It is particularly important to have children use headphones when working at the computer to avoid distracting other children.

- Keep classroom supplies in a consistent location.

- Regulate the classroom activity flow. Provide specific activities children can independently complete when finished with required work.

- If the room is not easily modified, another solution may be to create a place away from other children within the room with something like a separate carrel or study tent.

Area Screen

A section of a room can become a quiet seating area by using a screen to remove the visual distraction of other children. In the below illustration, a bookcase and commercially available three-foot folding screen visually isolate a chair. Having books in the bookcase allows children to read while seated but not to see other activity in the room.

The screen should be placed in a way that allows the teacher to always keep visual contact with children by looking over the screen from anywhere in the room. The screen may be attached to the wall with three secure brackets to make sure that it will not fall or be pulled down.

Bookcases could be used to create the same effect as in this Reading Center, but the screen has the advantage of allowing the teacher to fold it back so that the entire room can be utilized.

Note: You may need to verify that your school allows modification of the room and that it meets your school's safety requirements.

Classroom Environment

Seating Example

Seating Example

Simplifying the classroom environment and careful classroom seating arrangements such as placing desks in a horseshoe array can help lessen environmental distractions. Below is an example of a room where the teacher's desk is facing a semicircular grouping of children's desks. The fluorescent lighting in the room has been removed and lights have been placed along the ceiling to hang over each desk and provide a direct, non-glare light source for each child.

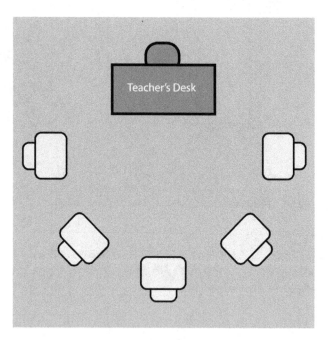

Note: You may need to verify that your school allows modification of the room and that it meets your school's safety requirements.

Chapter 2
Arousal Regulation & Attention

Children with special needs have difficulties regulating their actions and responses to their surroundings. Their lack of self-regulation, or ability to control themselves in a variety of environmental conditions, can lead to behavior problems. Self-regulation skills include: calming, delaying gratification, inhibiting responses, and maintaining an awareness of goals and how to alter behavior to attain a goal. Children may need help with maintenance of focused attention and interpreting their own mental states as well as those of others.

In a classroom, the behavior of children with special needs can be misinterpreted as being intentional. Behavior difficulties can be attributed to different factors and often are related to the inability to maintain self-control automatically and/or consciously.

OBSERVED BEHAVIOR	HOW THE BEHAVIOR IS LINKED TO SELF-REGULATION DIFFICULTIES
Aggressive	Inability to control actions, inability to control emotions
Cannot sit still	Over stimulated and cannot calm
Defiant	Inefficient intake, processing, and sustaining attention causing poor understanding
Impulsive	Inability to inhibit responses, poor planning, "in the moment" thinking
Inconsistent	Difficulty modulating energy according to task requirements
Unmotivated	Weakness sustaining consistent energy output

Aggressive

▶▶▶ **Strategies for helping children with aggression:**

- Use nonverbal cues to help redirect children before the situation escalates.

  Example: Physically hand a child another toy and ask him to show you how it works if the toy he has breaks.

  Example: Give a child a schedule and ask him what is next if he gets frustrated with what he is doing.

- Provide a quiet area and an escape route for children to have a place to go to regroup.

- Use social stories to help children understand the cause and effects of their actions and to instruct on appropriate social interactions.

Not Right to Bite

play with friends	I like to play with friends.	this is fun!
play my way!	Sometimes when I play with friends, I want them to play my way.	
I feel upset	Sometimes when my friends won't play my way, I feel upset.	
bite	When I feel upset I bite children. Children do not like it when I bite them.	
that hurts!	When I bite children it hurts them. When I bite children they don't want to play with me.	
listen to music	When I feel upset, instead of biting, I will listen to music to help me feel better.	
no biting	When I play with friends, I will not bite.	Good Job!

telephone   do not   go outside

○ *Stopping inappropriate behavior using story strips*
"Do no go outside while Mom is on the Phone"

Cannot Sit Still

▶▶▶**Strategies for helping children sit still:**

- Provide frequent activity breaks.

- Allow time for children to reorganize after high energy activities. Read a story or complete a quiet activity.

- Arrange with children that they will work for a specific length of time. Use a sand or visual timer to demonstrate the length of time. For example, children will work for four flips of the sand timer before a break. Teach children to use check marks or tally marks to keep track of the number of flips. Gradually increase the amount of flips or time length.

- During work periods have children sit on a T-stand to help direct energy and focus.

- Have children sit on a barrel seat - they can move on the seat without disturbing others.

- Have children sit on a balance disc cushion, an inflatable cushion with nubby bumps all over it.

A barrel turned upside down makes a stool that is not easily tilted

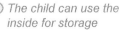

The child can use the inside for storage

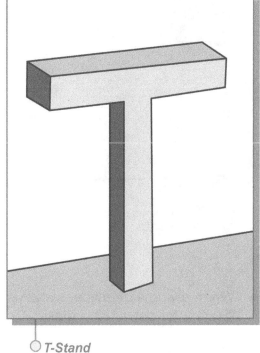

T-Stand

Defiant

▶▶▶**Strategies for helping children with defiance:**

- Limit choices.

  Example: Instead of asking "What toy do you want?" ask ,"Which of these two toys would you like to play with next?"

- Maintain consistent classroom expectations.

- Use a cue to direct children's attention before presenting the directions.

  Example: Hand children pictures showing what you will be discussing.

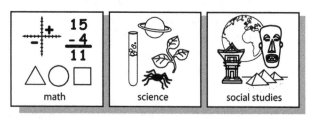

- Have children restate the directions in their own words to check for their understanding.

- Explicitly define the purpose of the lesson and/or child's expectation.

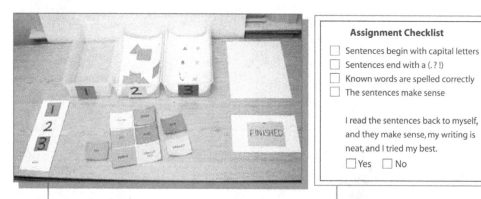

Numbered containers and finished folder provide task division for younger children.

Assignment Checklist
Explain what you expect on a writing assignment. Say, "Before you turn this into me, check that all the things on this list are complete."

- When giving a direction, avoid using phrases like, "I want you to ..." to limit the triggers for power struggles.

Impulsive

▶▶▶**Strategies for helping children with impulsivity:**

- Use simple and clearly defined requirements.

  Example: Say to children, "When we go to the store, always hold my hand."

- Use picture schedules to exhibit the actions requested.

- Maintain consistent schedule and classroom routines.

- Provide instruction to help the student learn to plan actions and their effects. Use self-talking strategies such as "If I know this... then..."

  Example of planning: "If I know where my cubbyhole is in the classroom, then I know where to put my coat."

  Example of cause/effect: "If I yell in class, I will have to sit in the quiet area."

- Teach children to count to ten before making a response.

- Use student self-rating systems and graphs to illustrate progress and accountability.*

School Weekly Morning Schedule The same activities every day of the week can limit impulsive actions from unexpected transitions.

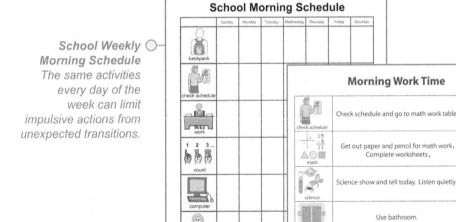

Morning Work Time Daily Schedule There is a column to check when done and a clock that you can put hands on to show the time this event will occur.

Inconsistent

▶▶▶**Strategies for helping children with inconsistent performance:**

- Present tasks in manageable pieces and clearly define the grading expectations.

  Example: Use rubrics to show children the assignment expectations. Describe to children how their reading assignment work is to be assessed. The example below shows the criteria for each component of a reading assignment: (1) determining the main idea; (2) noting important information; and (3) putting the information together.

Story Summary

EXPECTATION	BEGINNING	EMERGING	MASTERED
1. Main Idea	Provides irrelevant details to describe the passage.	Uses important details to tell what the passage is about, but has some misunderstandings.	Provide a succinct statement about the topic of the passage.
2. Important Information	Tells everything he knows about what he has read.	Describes using some of a story's frame word.	Tells about the main characters, events, problem, and/or solution.
3. Putting the information together to formulate a conclusion or summary	Disorganized presentation of the story that contains three or more misunderstandings.	Identifies beginning, middle, and end of a story, but leaves out one ore more important facts or details.	Uses the main idea, describes the story using beginning, middle, and end, and presents conclusions accurately.

Inconsistent

- Use checklists to help children plan and remember the steps to a task. This will help them to predict the length of the assignment.

  Example: Texts and image lists can help children plan and remember steps.

- Provide a quiet area for children to maintain attention and work pacing.

- Use mental management techniques to help children learn to regulate work pace and output.

	Homework Assignment	
MONTH of _____ Tuesday, April 2	**Homework for David A.**	This is fun!
+ 15 - 4 11 △◯▢ Math	**problems:**_____	
Reading	**read chapter:**_____ **answer questions:**_____	
Science	**complete worksheet** **on**_____	
Social Studies	**chapter** _____ **questions**	
	FINISHED! GREAT JOB!	

Arousal Regulation & Attention
Unmotivated

Unmotivated

▶▶▶ **Strategies for helping children with motivation:**

- Help children establish goals; this will help to engage children with the learning process.

  Example: *"When we finish our math, we can go outside and play".*

- Provide consistent feedback.

- Use genuine praise.

  Example: *Say to children, "I could tell that you understood the steps because you did all the steps to solve the problem."*

- Follow demanding tasks with assignments/tasks that children can complete successfully.

- Use acknowledgement for successful actions.

Put a colorful sticker on the assignment page when completed or for each step completed for complex tasks.

Friday Afternoon		
eat	☺ Good Job!	✓
swing	☺	✓
bathroom	☺ You did it!	✓
car		
bowling		
home		

Chapter 3
Behavior in the Classroom

All children need to be educated in a setting where they can feel safe and respected, where they can learn, and where they can develop socially and emotionally. However, behavioral disruptions can negatively affect the learning environment for children causing the disruptions as well as for the remaining children.

It is possible to manage behavioral disruptions effectively, allowing children presenting the behavioral problems to interact productively in the learning environment. However, there are a multitude of factors that could influence disruptive behavior in a classroom setting.

It is important to determine these influences in order to decide upon the level of intervention needed to support children. It is necessary to consider the children's needs in relation to the situation. Classroom modification strategies can provide the necessary support. However, some children require direct interventions, such as a Functional Behavioral Analysis (FBA), a behavior intervention plan, and/or therapeutic services.

A goal of behavior intervention is to guide children to learn to manage their behavior. A successful behavior intervention helps children to learn to be accountable for their actions by working with them to set goals and rewards. Also, frequent communication allows children to understand the purpose and reasons for the intervention.

Children's disruptive behaviors may be influenced by multiple factors. Working with professionals to determine the influences on the behaviors is an important step to devise an effective behavior plan.

Behavior in the Classroom
Behavioral Influences

Behavioral Influences

A variety of factors and influences can affect children's interactions in a group setting. Often, accommodations made within the classroom setting can help to support children who are struggling with maintaining acceptable behavior. Other times, children may require a more structured behavior intervention plan to provide a unified approach in the classroom setting.

Some of the elements that could impact children's abilities to interact appropriately in an educational setting include long-term influences such as cognitive functioning and developmental profiles. Other aspects of life that could affect behavior may be short-term such as moving to a new home, losing a family pet, and/or a minor illness that could cause temporary discomfort.

EXTERNAL INFLUENCES	INTERNAL INFLUENCES
» **Transitions or Changes at Home**	» **Unreasonable Expectations**
» **Unreasonable Expectations**	» **Cognitive Functioning**
» **Minor Illness/Discomfort**	» **Developmental Profile**
» **Death of a Family Member**	» **Communication Difficulties**
» **Loss of a Pet**	» **Individual's Temperament**
» **A New Family Member**	» **Emotional Problems**
» **Divorce and/or Remarriage of a Parent**	» **Learning Difficulties**
» **Abuse**	
» **Chronic or Serious Illness**	
» **Heavy Academic Demands**	
» **Inappropriate Educational Placement**	

Behavioral Influences

Because of the variety of factors that could impact children's behavior in an educational setting, it might be necessary for an interdisciplinary team that includes the classroom teacher, the special educator, the school counselor, the school psychologist, the behavior specialist, and the family to collaborate and determine the effective modes of behavior interventions.

However, in some cases, modifications and strategies implemented in the class setting might alleviate some of the behavior difficulties.

Given the variability of behavior difficulties, a child's individual case would need to be considered in order to devise an effective behavior management plan.

Children will respond to situations in different ways. An event that has a short-term effect on one child could have long-term influences on another child.

When you feel mad you can:		
1 2 3 ... count	Count to 10.	
	Do some jumping jacks.	
listen to music	Listen to music.	
	Tell your teacher how you are feeling.	

Determining Support Needs

1. Conduct a specific Behavioral Needs Assessment* to determine children's skills and challenges.
2. From the information gathered, attempt to determine the trigger to the behavior disruption.
3. Formulate a hypothesis to structure the behavior intervention.
4. Create a practical Behavior Management Plan** to eliminate the behavior.

Hypothesis:

CW becomes disruptive during task transitions. With support and preventive measures, he will improve his skills at maneuvering the classroom without disrupting the class.

He exhibits aggressive behaviors toward other children when he becomes anxious during the transitions.

CW has difficulties regulating his reactions to the classroom environment. His reactions are triggered when there are changes in the schedule, changes in activities, or during unstructured playtime.

The first step in conducting a Behavioral Needs Assessment is the creation of a hypothesis.

Classroom Expectations:

1. Keep hands to yourself.
2. Walk, don't run, when in the classroom.
3. Use words to tell when you are upset.

Target no more than three behaviors at a time.

* See Appendix "Classroom Observation Form"
** See Appendix "Behavior Management Form"

Behavior Needs Assessment

When observing a child's classroom behavior, use questions to guide the observation. This would assist in a developing the hypotheses to structure.

Examples of Guiding Questions:

- Are there noticeable patterns to the behaviors? Do the behaviors occur in relation to specific activities, types of tasks, or times of the day?

- Are there environmental factors that seem to precede the negative behaviors? Do the behaviors occur in a variety of settings?

- Are there other factors such a medical condition, experiencing acute or chronic pain, traumatic events, or the use of alcohol or other substances that could be impacting a child's behavior?

- Can a child's behavior be described or defined in useful terms to formulate an effective support plan?

- What are the teacher's reactions to the negative behaviors? What are the teacher's reactions to a child when they are inappropriately interacting in the classroom? Do the negative behaviors seem to fulfill a goal or purpose?

- Is the child aware of the inappropriate behavior? Can the child describe or explain feelings to help create an explanation of the occurrence?

- How does the child feel after a behavioral incident? Is the child able to talk about it once he has calmed down?

- How is the child treated by the teachers and by the other children after a behavioral outburst?

- Does the child understand the classroom expectations? Are the classroom expectations overwhelming for the child?

  Example: Ask a child before an action what he should be doing next. If there are guides for activities, see if he knows where they are and how to use them.

- How does the child communicate his needs, wants, and ideas to others? Does a child seem to have difficulties expressing his thoughts? Could this impact his interactions in the classroom and in what ways?

Behavior in the Classroom
Determining Support Needs

- How does the child perceive and/or interpret the classroom expectations?

- Does the child show signs indicating anxiety or other triggers that could indicate a behavioral outburst? Are there safeguards that can be implemented to prevent behavioral outbursts?

  Example: If a child loses control, he is sent to a quiet area of the room that is divided from the main classroom.

- Are there changes to the classroom environment that can help to support the child? If so, how can the changes be implemented?

- Does the child need additional assessment from a psychologist, school counselor, behavioral specialist, or another professional to help design an effective behavior plan?

- How can the school and the family work together to help support the child's behavior issues? Are there issues that need to be addressed outside of school to help the child?

  Example: Develop a communications plan with parents to keep the child's behavior reinforcements consistent between school and home.

After formulating the guiding questions, observe the child's behavior in the classroom.* Observations need to occur across different times of day in different settings, such as in the classroom and in the playground or in the lunch room. Pay close attention to the event or events that preceded the behavior.

Whenever possible, ask a neutral observer to conduct the behavioral assessment during class time.*

If this is not possible, try using a small slip of paper and pencil to mark the number of occurrences. Wait to transfer the number of occurrences to the data sheet until the end of the observation.

Keeping a sticky pad or small note pad handy for recording makes it less obvious to the children that a behavioral observation is occurring. This will promote a more natural interaction in the classroom.

---

* See Appendix "Teacher Observation Form"

Behavior Needs Assessment

From the data gathered, conclusions and interventions can be created to address the disruptive behaviors or to help with discovering if additional services are needed to support children in their educational setting.

ANTECEDENTS THAT COULD TRIGGER NEGATIVE BEHAVIOR

» **Hearing "No!" frequently**

» **Direction to stop an action without presenting a replacement action**

Example: Provide activities that are related to the lesson but that the children enjoy doing, such as art projects.

» **Harshly stated commands**

» **Language and gestures that are interpreted as showing disapproval**

Example: Take out personal phrases like "I want..." Use "You need to..." or "It is time to..." or "We need to..."

» **Too much praise that may not be interpreted as genuine**

» **Too much unstructured or idle time**

Art projects are a great way to keep children engaged and occupied after they have completed their work.

Behavior in the Classroom
Behavior Management Plan

Behavior Management Plan*

If unsure of the reasons for behavior problems, you may choose to do a Behavior Needs Assessment first. Some problems can be solved by simpler solutions, such as changes within the classroom strategies.

Steps to Create a Behavior Management Plan:

1. Create a list of goals to target problem behaviors.

2. Define replacement behaviors for the targeted behaviors.

3. Use feedback to reinforce use of replacement behaviors.

4. Define the teacher monitoring methods.

5. Follow through and phase out the monitoring.

6. Communicate with the family to coordinate efforts.

- Keep the behavior expectations simple.

- Post the rules and refer to them often.

- Provide children with an acceptable replacement behavior.

- Establish a preventive signal system if possible – use the preventive signal once as a reminder.

   Example signals are:
   --Stand in front of desk
   --Hold up a visual cue card
   --Tap finger on desk
   --Touch child's shoulder

- Provide immediate feedback.

- Initiate consequences as soon as possible once the disruption occurs.

- Make sure the consequence is related to the incident.

* See Appendix "Behavior Management Form"

Goals

Children need to have a small set of easily defined goals to help direct their behavior. Prioritize the goals and select the behaviors that present the most difficulty. Limit the Behavior Management Plan to address no more than three behaviors at a time. Clearly state each behavior goal as an improvement goal or outcome to help motivate a child's participation in the process.

Example: A child will stay with the activity until the teacher directs the child to another activity.

GOALS:

1. CW will not become disruptive during task transitions.
2. CW will not exhibit aggressive behaviors toward other children when he becomes anxious.
3. CW will regulate his reactions to the classroom environment.

In the Sample Behavior Management Plan, three goals are chosen for an imaginary child called CW, whose reactions are triggered when there are changes in the schedule, changes in classroom routines and during unstructured play time.

Replacement Behaviors

Determine behaviors that will help a child accomplish the goals defined in Step 1 of the Behavior Management Plan. The replacement behaviors need to match the developmental level of the child.

Example: A child who hits other children when angry may need to practice a replacement behavior of clasping his hands behind his back when angry.

Target replacement behaviors are chosen for CW based on the goals. These replacement strategies may or may not directly match the 3 goals in Step 1, since actions such as going to a quiet area when upset can be a replacement strategy for more than one goal, and one goal can have several replacement actions.

REPLACEMENT BEHAVIORS:

1. Signal to teacher when overwhelmed.
2. Use words when angry.
3. Keep hands to yourself. Keep hands away from other children when angry.
4. Learn to go to a quiet area independently when needing to calm down.
5. Go to an adult to ask for help when transitions or peer negotiations are difficult.

Behavior in the Classroom
Behavior Management Plan

Student Feedback

Communicate to children what behaviors you want changed and why. When asking children to change behaviors, it is important to help them understand that rules and expectations are to keep them and others safe in a classroom. Many times children feel that rules are set to make their lives miserable. The adults need to reiterate that rules are made for a reason other than annoyance.

Briefly provide children with the reason for the appropriate behavior, but do not negotiate or argue with the children once a rule or expectation has been established. This will help to establish a clear boundary for the behavior expectation.

Feedback needs to be given to the children consistently and immediately. Types of feedback presented to the children need to be based upon their developmental profile, their cognitive functioning, their emotional status, and according to their responses or reactions to different forms of praise, rewards, and consequences.

WHEN DISCUSSING THE BEHAVIOR PLAN WITH THE STUDENT

» **Use clear and simple statements.**

» **Explain to the children what the expectations are going to be and how you are going to help them adapt to using a more appropriate behavior.**

» **Provide guidance to help children use the appropriate replacement behavior.**

» **Outline the type of feedback that will be used.**

» **Discuss the type of rewards and consequences that will be used. Make it immediate and relevant.**

» **Make sure the behavior expectations, the replacement behavior, and the feedback are developmentally appropriate.**

Example: "Stand in line quietly, and we can get to lunch quickly." A consequence specific to the behavior is, "If it is too difficult to stand with your hands to yourself, you will need to stand by me so I can help you."

STUDENT FEEDBACK:

1. CW responds well to acknowledgement. Use statements to connect the positive actions and provide verbal recognition when he is meeting his goals.

2. A desk chart will be created with stickers to reward replacement behavior. If CW receives three stickers at the end of the day, he will be able to select a favorite activity from the reward survey to complete during activity time.

3. If CW does not meet the criteria of three stickers at the end of the day, the teacher will present him with choices of activities to select during unstructured time, or he may need to use that time to make up the work he missed.

4. Story boards and discussions will be utilized with CW to discuss the behavior incident as soon as he is able to discuss the problem. With the aid of the instructor, the problem will be reviewed and supportive options for next time created.

5. If CW cannot transition without assistance, a teacher will facilitate class changes. This may involve using tools such as handing CW a visual card to demonstrate transition time.

6. Time out intervention will be taught. If CW refuses to interact appropriately, he will be directed away from the current activity. He will need to make up at another time any academic instruction he missed. This may have to occur during an unstructured time. However, it should not take up the entire free time period.

7. Natural consequences, such as using a waiting chair, will be used as much as possible. Care should be taken not to embarrass the child by singling him out for punishment.

The Sample Behavior Management Plan describes feedback that targets CW's way of interacting.

Behavior in the Classroom
Behavior Management Plan

Praise & Rewards

It may be beneficial, especially with older children, to conduct a rewards survey to determine what may motivate them toward utilizing the appropriate behavior. The survey can be something as simple as watching which rewards children enjoy, or a more formal survey where you list or show all possible rewards and note the choices over time.

If using a reward-based behavior management plan, gradually phase out giving rewards as the negative behaviors become less frequent. Provide genuine praise or acknowledgement when children use appropriate behavior or when children are able to control the negative behavior.

When giving acknowledgement directly state the positive action.

Example: "You were really thoughtful when you stepped back from children who was pushing in line".

Pointing out to children when they interact in ways that show self-awareness helps them to understand acceptable behaviors. This models the use of the appropriate behaviors.

- Some children have difficulties interpreting the verbal and nonverbal cues that are given during exchanges.

- Some children could misinterpret the message when verbal and nonverbal signals are inconsistent.

Example: Don't say "Good job" in a flat, uninterested voice or put your hands on your hips while saying "Good job".

- Make sure the verbal message is consistent with the facial expression or body position.

Example: Say "Good job" and smile while clapping your hands. When using the phrase "good job" link it closely to the task. For example, " Good job (clap your hands) putting the papers in the bin."

Consequences and Corrections

Consequences and corrections need to be meaningful, immediate, and related to the inappropriate behavior. For example, if children do not complete their assignments before participating in a free choice activity, such as computer time, then computer time needs to be removed from activity choice. When discussing the inappropriate behavior and the consequence with children, it is important to communicate how the behavior impacts their learning or interactions in the classroom.

It is important to analyze the possible cause of the inappropriate behavior in relation to the children's ability, the task or situation demands, to the appropriateness of the request made on children. This will help to determine if there are possible learning difficulties, misunderstanding of directions, or confusion that would impact behavior. These issues impact the type of consequence or correction children require.

Provide special types of seating arrangement to quiet or calm down areas of the room.

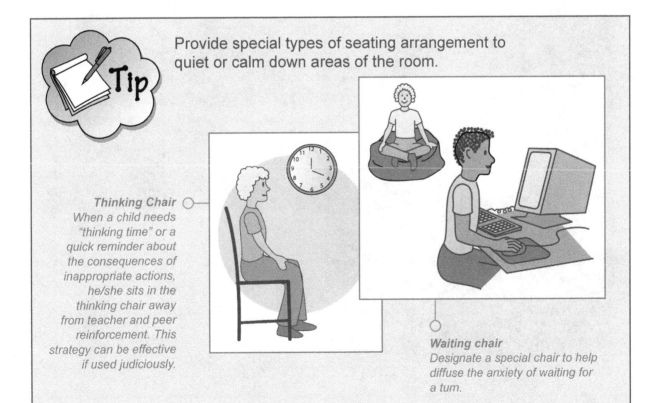

Thinking Chair
When a child needs "thinking time" or a quick reminder about the consequences of inappropriate actions, he/she sits in the thinking chair away from teacher and peer reinforcement. This strategy can be effective if used judiciously.

Waiting chair
Designate a special chair to help diffuse the anxiety of waiting for a turn.

Behavior in the Classroom
Behavior Management Plan

When selecting consequences, try to avoid using recess time if possible. Recess is a valuable learning time for children. It provides opportunities to use motor skills to reorganize thoughts, apply learning in a natural situation, and practice social skills.

Also, avoid adding extra homework assignments or additional class work as a behavioral consequence. This could attach a negative connection to the learning process. When this occurs, children often become focused on the issue of the additional assignment and not on the purpose of the task or the quality of their output.

Visual Feedback

Visual cues and reminders are an invaluable tool for behavior management. Charts and cues need to be developed according to the children's needs.

USING A BEHAVIOR CHART*

Flower Chart Directions:

1. Use the flower chart during an activity to monitor the interactions.

2. Establish that a child must have 1 petal on the flower in order to get a simple reinforcement, such as a sticker.

3. If a child does not follow the expectation, a petal is not given.

4. If a child does not have a petal after the activity period, then he/she does not receive a reinforcement for that activity.

5. A child must receive three stickers by the end of the day in order to receive a positive reinforcement at home after school.

Name: _____

Behavior in the Classroom
Behavior Management Plan

Monitoring Older Students

Older children may not respond to visual charts. Some older children respond to self-monitoring or self-rating approaches where they are required to reflect upon their interactions at school.

Older children still require specific expectations, explanations of the goals and purposes of using the appropriate behaviors, and reminders about the appropriate behaviors. The information gathered from self-rating scales can be presented in a graph form to children. This can provide the visual demonstration of their progress and entice the older student to participate in the process.

Name: Sandra   Date: December 10

Using a scale from 3 to 1, rate how you did in each class.
3 = great
2 = ok
1 = oops

Target	MATH	Language Arts	GYM	Science
Waited for teacher to finish talking before responding	3	2	3	3
Counted to 10 and thought about my answer before responding	1	1	2	2
Used appropriate tone of voice	3	2	2	3

How would you describe your performance today?

OKay.

Was it harder to meet the targets in some classes more than others? Why or why not?

Languge arts class was hard because there are too many students.

What do you think would help you next time?

If Mrs. Carl would talk slower, I would listen much better.

A Self-Monitoring Sheet* is a useful tool for older children.

Self-Monitoring Sheet Data Results

Self-Monitoring Behavior Data

Week of: December 10

Target	Math	Language Arts	Physical Education	Science
Waited to respond until teacher finished talking.	15	10	7	9
Counted to 10 and thought about the reply before responding to the teacher or to another student.	8	12	5	12
Used an appropriate tone of voice for the situation.	14	11	5	14

The data are added for 5 days to create a total count.

The higher number (15) is the goal for each behavior. This indicates the student has mastered the behavior.

Self-Monitoring Sheet Visual Graph of Results

Methods to Monitor Behavior

Once you determine the method of feedback that will be most effective, develop a schedule for monitoring the behavior. For younger children, this may need to be on a daily or even class period basis with visual techniques like desk charts and flower charts. For older children, weekly self-assessments may be sufficient.

The teacher may also keep separate checklists and notes that are not shown to children for personal reference. This summary can be helpful in communicating progress with parents and therapists.

MONITORING BEHAVIOR:

1. Behavior will be monitored on a daily basis.
2. Tally charts using a desk chart form will be recorded by CW and collected each day and discussed.
3. Behavioral interventions will be monitored through teacher checklists, observations, and anecdotal notes.
4. Information will be summarized on a weekly basis.

In the Sample Behavior Management Plan, four methods for monitoring CW's behavior are chosen.

A desk chart* is a way to monitor student progress on a behavior goal.

Desk Chart

Name: **Sandra**   Date: **Monday**

Action	1	2	3	Sticker
Tell teacher when overwhelmed	✓			
Use words when angry	✓	✓	✓	🙂
Keep hands to yourself				
Go to a quiet area to calm down	✓			
Ask for help when changes or other students bother you	✓	✓		

Behavior in the Classroom
Behavior Management Plan

Family Communication *

When working with a Behavior Management Plan, it is important to collaborate with a child's family. Frequent communication with the home can help provide feedback about using the appropriate behavior. Also, it can help to minimize confusion about incidents that occurred at school.

COMMUNICATION SUGGESTIONS

» **Determine the type of information that would be most useful to support a child in both the family and educational settings.**

» **Establish a point person at school to direct and respond to the communications. The point person could be the lead teacher or a school counselor. It needs to be someone who works closely with the child and understands the issues.**

» **Decide how the communications between home and school need to be sent (e.g. Email, notes, telephone calls, folders carried by children).**

» **Decide how often the communications need to be passed between home and school.**

In the Sample Behavior Management Plan, family communication includes these points.

FAMILY COMMUNICATION:

1. Daily notes will be sent in CW's communication or school folder.

2. A weekly summary of the behavior will be emailed to the family.

3. Information sent to CW's family will include how often he signaled the instructor, the effectiveness of the redirection, and the use of the tally and sticker system.

4. A weekly summary will consist of the current week's progress and will compare to prior weeks. It will note any intervention changes.

---

* See Appendix: *"Conference Log", "Communication Log", and "Dear Parents Letter"*

Establishing a consistent communication system with families is necessary to support children. Also, it demonstrates to children that their instructors and the caregivers are working in a unified manner.

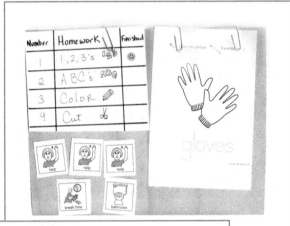

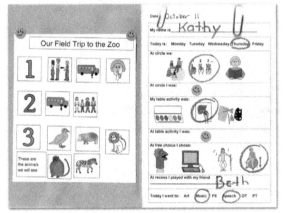

○ *School Work Communication Folder*
This is an example of a school work communication folder. All the information that is needed to get the task done is organized and listed here. Handy for homework and classroom work, communication folders are wonderful for building independence.

» *Works best using a plastic colored folder for durability.*

» *Attach work assignment with appropriate explanations, and a place to check when finished, on the left page.*

» *Attach worksheets on facing page in order, attached with paper clips.*

» *Picture cards for asking help, requesting break, or bathroom are attached with Velcro and available at the bottom.*

○ *Daily Communication Folder*
This is an example of a communication folder that explains what happened during the day. These can bridge the gap between home and school activities. Pre-made forms can be given to children to be filled out independently or with a teacher's help. Use at school on a daily or weekly basis or make some "home activity" forms that explain weekend activities for children to share at school. Example content includes:

» *Child's name at the top*
» *Day of week*
» *Center time activities*
» *Special classes*
» *Free time choices*
» *Name of a friend played with*

The options are endless and can be designed with specific communication goals in mind.

Behavior in the Classroom
Behavior Management Plan

Follow Through and Phase Out

The behavior plan implemented at school should be discussed with a child's psychologist or mental health service provider. The providers would be able to assist in the process.

Follow up meetings need to be convened periodically to review the implementation of the plan and the effectiveness. This may need to occur every 3 to 6 weeks. Changes to the plan or to the interventions need to be discussed at that time (e.g., phasing out rewards).

Once children have effectively reached the goals in the Behavior Management Plan, the feedback and monitoring would need to be phased out gradually. If the support tools, such as Self-Monitoring Sheets or desk charts, are removed too quickly, children may revert to the problem behaviors. Even with gradual removal of rewards and reminders, some children may need continual reminders, such as schedules and visuals, to help organize activities and control behaviors.

FOLLOW THROUGH:

1. The family has indicated they are working with a therapist on self-regulation and behavior management at home. Therapy is focusing on helping CW recognize feelings and select appropriate responses. The therapist will consult and work with CW's instructors to help maintain a consistent management plan and interventions.

2. Biweekly emails with CW's therapist will occur to review CW's progress and make necessary adjustments to his behavior plan.

3. A meeting with parents, teachers, and therapists will be convened in four weeks to review progress and adjust the behavior plan if necessary.

4. When CW reaches his goals, a method for phase out will be determined based on the time he took to learn the behaviors and his dependency on each particular feedback technique.

The Sample Behavior Management Plan includes a plan for following through and phasing out .

Classroom Strategies

Many of the behavior incidents can be handled with simple changes and accommodations. Children are learning about their place in the world, and they require room to make mistakes and to grow in a safe environment. Maintaining a sense of humor can help when creating effective learning situations.

CHRONIC MISUNDERSTANDING OF VERBAL DIRECTIONS

- Slow the rate of speaking.

- Use visual cues to help with the explanation.

- Use simple statements.

- Have children paraphrase to check understanding.

- Limit movement when presenting directions to give a consistent sound projection.

CHRONIC MISUNDERSTANDING OF NONVERBAL CUES

- Make sure that the verbal message matches with the nonverbal signals when talking with children.

  Example: Don't smile at children when correcting bad behavior.

- Provide direct instruction on how to notice what body position, vocal intonation, and gestures imply. Children with special needs may confuse gestures and need to have the meanings explicitly explained.

  Example: Tell a child that when you look at him and place your hands on your hips and shake your head left to right, it means that what he is doing is wrong and he needs to stop doing it.

- Provide practice understanding nonverbal cues in a non-threatening environment. Since nonverbal cues are usually linked to physical responses from others, they can be stressful.

RANDOMLY MOVING FROM ONE ACTIVITY TO ANOTHER WITHOUT FINISHING

- Use visual checklists or picture directions to lay out instructions and expectations.*

- Limit the number of activity centers or choices.

- Specify the sequence of activities children need to follow. Use picture schedules to help children follow the sequence.

- Define what needs to be done before beginning another activity.

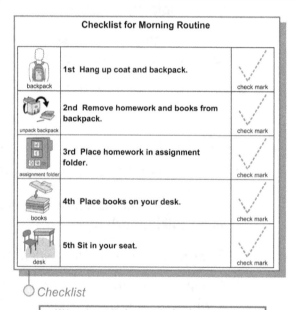

David's Monday Schedule

hang up jacket	Get ready for class	sit at desk
show and tell	Show the class something special you brought from home	
desk work	Work at your desk on what the teacher give's you to do	
lunch	Get your lunchbox and eat what is in it	lunch box
recess	Go outside and play with class	
story time	Sit on mat and listen to teacher read a story	sit on mat
time to play	Play until Mom comes to pick you up	

○ *Example picture directions for class day schedule*

Checklist for Morning Routine

backpack	1st Hang up coat and backpack.	check mark
unpack backpack	2nd Remove homework and books from backpack.	check mark
assignment folder	3rd Place homework in assignment folder.	check mark
books	4th Place books on your desk.	check mark
desk	5th Sit in your seat.	check mark

○ *Checklist*

Write a Journal to keep track of each task you do. For each task,
1. Does your journal entry include who, what, where, and when for the task? _____
2. Does your journal entry have a beginning, middle, and end step for the task? _____
3. Did you write in full sentences? _____
4. Did you use capitalization and punctuation? _____
5. Did you read your journal out loud? _____
6. Does your entry make sense? _____

○ *Example Journal to keep track of tasks*

Pick one free period activity:

listen to music   color

○ *Example of a choice limit*

---

* See Appendix: "Classroom Picture Cards"

DIFFICULTIES MAINTAINING APPROPRIATE DISTANCE FROM ANOTHER STUDENT WHILE STANDING IN LINE

- Place a marker or direct children to locate a landmark to help judge the appropriate space.

- Have children with behavior issues stand at the end or at the beginning of the line to limit the amount of spatial factors needed to understand acceptable distances between people.

DIFFICULTIES STANDING STILL WHILE STANDING IN LINE

- Place a white board or magnet board in the waiting area. Guide children to create sentences, words, or designs using the material.

- Engage children in a constructive task without bothering other children. Try to keep children active and busy.

Have children hold something to stay still

Behavior in the Classroom

Strategies

CONSTANT TALKING

- Seat children in a location with minimal distractions.

- Use a visual cue or "talking gauge" that can be moved to show when talking is too much without competing with or adding to the noise.

- Use a gentle touch on the shoulder to help as a reminder.

- Have children keep a notebook when they feel they must talk but it is inappropriate. Encourage them to write down their thoughts and allow another time for them to present their thoughts.

○ *Make a Talking Gauge*

1. Take a paper plate and cut it in half.

2. Attach a pointer using a paper clip.

3. Write on the left side "Too Quiet". Write in the center "Just Right", and on the right side of the half write "Too Loud!"

The teacher then can place the gauge in a visible location and direct children to notice its location. The teacher can use the gauge to indicate to a child when there is too much talking and help to draw his/her attention back to the lesson. Training a child to watch the teacher moving the gauge will help him/her to learn to be aware to the surroundings and to adjust behavior accordingly.

DIFFICULTIES WAITING TO BE CALLED ON IN CLASS

- Be specific when children are going to be called upon.

  Example: *"After I call on Johnny, I am going to call on you."*

- Establish at the beginning of the school year the importance of raising the hand and waiting to be called to contribute. Hand children a visual card for raising a hand as a reminder if they forget.

- State the importance of wanting to hear the ideas of every student and the benefits from learning from each other.

- Ignore children who call out and select another to answer the question.

DIFFICULTIES STAYING IN THE SEAT

- Have children sit on a stool or T-stand to help redirect their attention to their desk and work.

- Provide opportunities for children to move without disturbing others.

- Allow children to use a lapboard and work on the floor.

- Have children work at a table to provide room for movement.

CONSTANTLY NEEDING TO LEAVE THE ROOM

- Allot specific times to get a drink of water.

  Example: *"You can get a glass of water after 30 minutes of work". Set visual timer to 30 minutes.*

  Example: *"You can get a glass of water after completing three steps on your schedule."*

- Specify days when children can perform errands.

- Clearly outline the expectations. Do not negotiate with children about leaving the room (excluding emergencies).

Math Class Work Schedule	
	Put your name and date on the top of a clean piece of paper.
	Copy the first four problems from Chapter 3 to the paper.
	Do the first 2 problems and write the answers on the paper.
	Raise your hand quietly until the teacher comes to your desk.

Behavior in the Classroom

Strategies

FREQUENTLY LOSING ITEMS FOR CLASS

- Have a general area for basic supplies. Keep pencils and paper available. Keep an additional set of books in the class.

- Keep room neat and organized. Have children partake in the clean up at the end of each day. This will help them to become aware of the location of the materials in the room.

- Toy shelves need to stay neat and organized. Tape a photo of the toy on the shelf to help children remember where items go after use.

- Provide children their own spaces to store book bags, lunch boxes, and extra clothes. Each cubby is labeled with the child's name and/or photograph.

FORGETTING TO TURN IN ASSIGNMENTS

- Establish a routine to turn in homework. Have student place assignments in the "in" basket as they enter the classroom.

- Use a weekly syllabus when assigning homework. Send a copy to the families each week and post one in the classroom.

- Maintain a homework routine. Keep homework routines simple and manageable.

- Establish an organizational system with children. Provide assistance until the children can manage the system independently.

Use a Homework Chart* to keep children organized

Homework Chart							December 2
	Sunday	Monday	Tuesday	Wednesday	Thursday	Friday	Saturday
MATH	Problems 1-4	Pages 36-42	Pages 43-58	Problems 1-4	Pages 59-68	Pages 69-70	
Language Arts		Spelling	Pages 24-35	Spelling	Pages 42-44	Spelling Test	
Reading		Read for 20 minutes	Read for 20 minutes	Read for 20 minutes	Read for 20 minutes	Read for 20 minutes	

* See Appendix "Homework Chart"

DIFFICULTIES MAINTAINING AN EFFICIENT WORK PACE IN SCHOOL

- Use sand or visual timers to help children experience specific lengths of times. Have children select how many flips of the sand timer before there is a break or show hands on a manual clock for when deadline is complete. Gradually increase the length of time before there is a break.

- Print and use a visual clock.*

- Lessen the length of an assignment. Grade assignments on accuracy rather than the amount of completion.

- Break large assignments into manageable tasks. Establish with children the goal to complete the assignment. Set check times to have selections completed if the children are able to work within time constraints.

- Use rubrics to provide a reminder of the expectation of the assignment. Present tasks in manageable pieces. Clearly define the grading expectations.

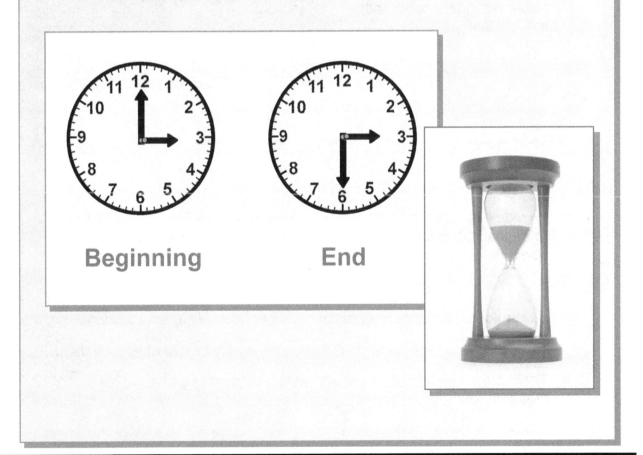

Beginning   **End**

LACK OF MOTIVATION

- Clearly define the purpose of the lesson.

- Follow difficult tasks with tasks that children enjoy or can complete successfully.

- Alternate types of tasks. Follow paper and pencil assignments with an active task.

- Have children participate in selecting topics of studies or materials to use. For older children, you can have them create their own schedules. Even older children may enjoy visual reminders rather than straight text.

	Afternoon Work Time	
cubbies	After lunch is over, put your empty lunch box in your cubby.	check mark
social studies	Get out your Social Studies book and read chapter 8.	check mark
Lincoln	Abe Lincoln, a character from history, will be visiting our class today. Listen quietly while he tells the class a story about his life.	check mark
raise hand	If you have a question for Mr. Lincoln, raise your hand until he calls on you.	check mark
write	Write a paragraph about what you learned about Abe Lincoln's role in history.	check mark
recess	Time for recess! Line up outside the door.	check mark
happy	Have fun playing outside.	check mark

DIFFICULTIES RESPONDING IN CLASS

- Provide extra time for children to respond to a question. Allow children more than 10 seconds to gather a response before providing prompts or selecting another.

- Give children a signal before calling on them.

  Example: *Stand in front of his/her desk before calling on a student.*

  Example: *Touch children on the shoulder lightly before calling on them.*

- Teach other children to be patient while a student is gathering his thoughts.

DIFFICULTIES WITH PLANNING

- Use meta-cognitive techniques and instruction to help children learn to be aware of the learning process. For older children, forms such as a self-monitoring sheet* can be used to understand the process of learning new material. For younger children, a desk chart* can visually explain how the parts of learning tie together. These tools can be used for learning material, not just behavioral replacement.

- Guide children to connect an assignment with something they already know or with something that looks familiar. Then have them scan the assignment to see what they need to do. After they have scanned and analyzed the tasks, encourage them to ask themselves if they are able to do the assignment or if they have questions.

- Teach children to use self-talk and guide them to make a plan, do the task, and review their process for each task or activity.

PATIENCE IN THE CLASSROOM

- Teach children about the differences in thinking styles and processes. For young children, story strips can be useful. For older children, writing a story where they pretend to be another person may help them see why someone acts as they do.

- Encourage children to think about their own learning processes and their own strengths and challenges.

- Help children to become their own advocate as well as to develop patience when working with other children with a variety of learning profiles.

- Reiterate that school is a place where all kids can learn in a respectful and safe environment.

Story strips are a way of visually describing another person's thinking.

Why did Zach hit Sam?

Zach was standing in line when Sam pushed him.
That made Zach angry, and he started yelling and hit Sam.

---

* See Appendix "Self-Monitoring Sheet" & "Desk Chart"

Chapter 4
Social Interactions

To be successful during social exchanges, children need to be able to understand the nonverbal cues and the social language or discourse that occur during interactions. Often these are subtle, fleeting signals that require children to process and interpret rapidly presented information in order to formulate a response.

Difficulties with social interactions may be influenced by difficulties with self-regulation, processing weaknesses, problems with analyzing spatial information, and weaknesses in cognitive flexibility.

Children need guidance to learn social skills in a safe and nurturing environment. If a child needs redirection or correction, try to avoid embarrassment and possible teasing by other children.

SOCIAL SUPPORTS FOR CHILDREN WITH SPECIAL NEEDS IN THE CLASSROOM

» Provide frequent adult assistance and facilitation during social or unstructured class periods. This will allow time to instruct children on how to interact successfully.

» Structure class activity time by providing the choices children can make. This will establish a framework and give some direction to an unstructured activity.

» Structure the classroom to enable children to navigate within the classroom. For example, keep desks and student locations away from high traffic areas to prevent accidental bumping into other students or other incidental student exchanges.

» Establish a classroom guideline that teasing and excluding classmates from classroom activities are not acceptable.

» Work with social stories in the classroom.*

See Appendix "Behavior Picture Cards"

Nonverbal Cues

Often children with special needs have problems recognizing the nonverbal cues and interpreting the meaning embedded in the signals. They may have difficulties recognizing personal space, linking vocal intonation with a facial expression to understand a person's feelings, and understanding gestures, such as a palm facing forward to mean stop. Some children require direct instruction to interpret the nonverbal cues that occur during social exchanges.

NONVERBAL CUES USED DURING SOCIAL INTERACTIONS
<ul><li>» **Body postures**</li><li>» **Personal space and spatial boundaries**</li><li>» **Facial expressions**</li><li>» **Gestures that co-occur with speech**</li><li>» **Personal dress**</li></ul> 

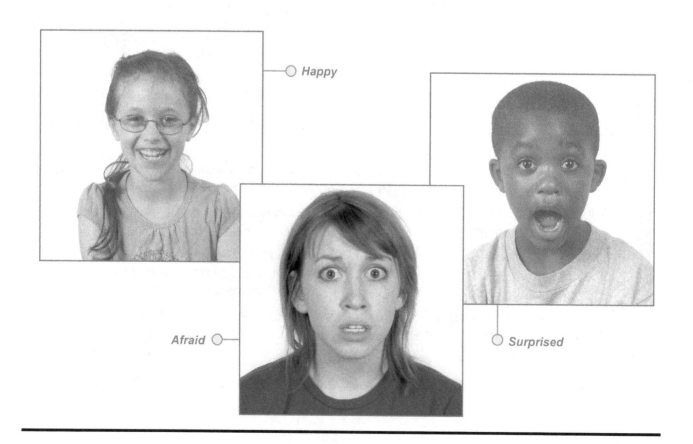

Happy

Afraid

Surprised

Children with special needs may benefit from support to help them process and understand nonverbal cues.

- Direct children to notice the facial expression and body posture during interactions. Use gentle verbal prompts such as, "What do you think my face is saying to you ?" to help point out the cues.

- Use colored markers to indicate standing space and distance to stand in line. Put a colored dot on a wall to indicate where children need to stand.

- Role-play in small groups to practice recognition of meaning conveyed in posturing and vocal intonations.

- Provide opportunities to have children watch short clips of videotapes of a television show with the sound off. Ask children what they think is happening by analyzing the postures and the movements of the actors.

- Play charades or pantomimes. Have children guess the message. This helps to draw attention to meaning in body posturing.

- Cue children to recognize common hand signs that are used in a classroom, such as recognizing the palm facing forward to mean stop, and the hands on the hips to convey displeasure.

Social Interactions
Social Discourse

Social Discourse

Some children with special needs may demonstrate relative strengths in their ability to retell an experience, to talk about a favorite subject, to make a comment, to state their needs and wants, and to answer basic questions.

However, children with special needs may have difficulties understanding the subtle nuances conveyed during conversations, maintaining the thread of the conversation because of difficulties with encoding and speed of processing, and overlooking the message that is presented through speech and gestures.

- In a small group setting, practice with children the meaning of words using different vocal intonations. This will help children recognize the differences in meaning caused by vocal changes.

- Play games that practice the speed of speech. Have children say something slowly. Have children say it fast. Have them change the rate of speech as you call out instructions.

- Encourage children to listen to others during discussion. Use a talking stick or another object and pass it around when talking about a topic. Establish the rule that a person can only speak when they have the talking stick in their hands. This helps to practice listening, waiting turns, and thinking about a topic before speaking; also it can help cue children to plan instead of quickly reacting.

- Have children count to 10 slowly (or backwards) before making a response. While counting, this provides time for them to register what the other person has said, and they can prepare a response.

- Play non-competitive games to help children learn to listen and exchange information. For example, basic card games such as "Go Fish" can be used during activities to practice waiting turns, listening, and formulating a response.

Children need to learn the skills to regulate their reactions to a comment or an action. With appropriate adult facilitation, direction instruction, guidance, and supervision, children with special needs can learn to interact in a variety of social situations

Uncaring

Children with special needs may appear at times to not care about the feelings of others. Activities can encourage empathy or help identify emotions

- Direct children to become aware of body language including stance, arm placement, and facial expression. When discussing an incident with children, encourage them to think how they would feel in that situation.

    Example: The last parts of the Feelings game links incidents with the feelings associated with them.

- Link the cause and effects to the actions.

- Practice using role playing games/scenarios to teach appropriate social skills.

- Have children work with the school counselor on social skills training.

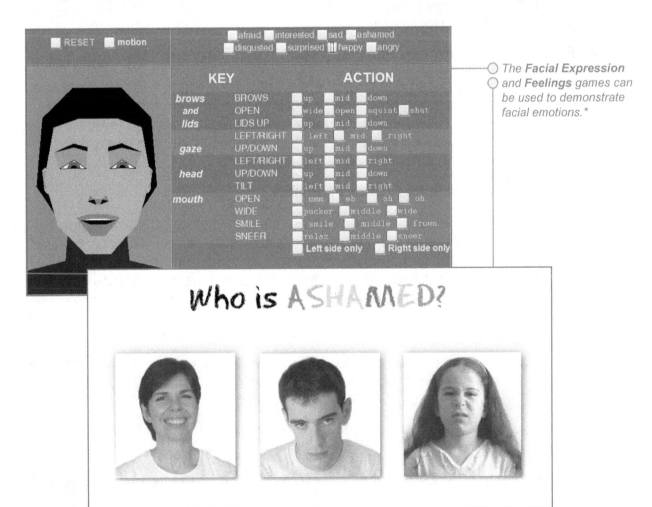

The *Facial Expression* and *Feelings* games can be used to demonstrate facial emotions.*

Social Play Action Figures*

Use characters customized with face photos for each child to teach listening, taking turns, staying on subject, and empathy.

- **Learn about the other students in class.**

  Let each child take home everyone's figures for one evening to play with and learn the faces and names. If you feel there might be a problem with children not returning all the figures, you can have each child take only his or her figure home and role play with imaginary figures created in class using faces from cartoons, clip art, or downloaded from the web. These characters used at home can help generalize the skills to new people outside the classroom.

- **Role play in pairs for learning turn taking, listening, and staying on topic.**

  Put children in pairs and set a timer at the front of the room. Let each child use his action figure to explain to his partner's action figure what he did that morning before school. Set timer to five minutes and when time is up, the person listening has to ask one question about the other's morning and the first person can answer for a minute. Then switch turns.

- **Role play in pairs to learn about empathy.**

  After a pair has role played for turn taking, have the two children exchange figures. Each person will pretend to be his partner's action figure and will describe what he thinks will happen getting ready for school tomorrow or after school today. Use the timer again to limit each person's time and let the two kids discuss how they felt about the other person's description of their life. You may want to allow a few minutes for each person to play the part, time for discussion after each person has taken his turn, and time at the end for answering questions like:

  » *Did you feel like you were in the other person's house (or class, or whatever is related to the scenario you set) when you were playing with his figure?*
  » *What did it feel like to be the other person?*
  » *Do you have any questions about his home, or whatever is related to the scenario he played?*

- Use a timer to allow each person to only talk a set time before the other person can talk.

Chapter 5
Classroom Rights

IDEA

Laws in many countries have been enacted to guarantee certain learning protections for children with special needs. While legislation is diverse, often changing, and implementation varies, IDEA provides one example of such an act in the United States.

INDIVIDUALS WITH DISABILITIES EDUCATION IMPROVEMENT ACT (IDEA) / INDIVIDUALIZED EDUCATION PROGRAM (IEP)

On December 3, 2004, the Individuals with Disabilities Education Improvement Act was enacted. This law revised the 1997 Individuals with Disabilities Education Act (IDEA) and specifically connects the rules for special education to the regulations determined by the 2003 No Child Left Behind Act (NCLB).

Children who are deemed eligible to receive special education services under their state and federal guidelines have an Individualized Education Program (IEP) that directs their learning program in the classroom.

Caregivers interested in finding out more information about the IEP process need to consult with their child's instructor, school counselor, lead special education teacher, or principal about the procedures in their school district. Though schools need to be in compliance with the federal IDEA law, some procedures vary according to state and district rules.

Classroom Rights
Program Elements

When devising an educational program for a child with special needs, it is important to consider the laws and their implementation within your school system. Broad areas often addressed by individual programs include:

ENVIRONMENT

- » **Opportunities for small group instruction in challenging academic areas**
- » **Opportunities for adult assistance and support**
- » **Feeling safe in the classroom**

INSTRUCTIONAL METHODS

- » **Developmentally appropriate instruction**
- » **Remedial interventions when needed**
- » **Adult facilitation to support challenging areas**

THERAPIES / EDUCATIONAL SUPPORTS

- » **Speech and language therapy**
- » **Occupational therapy**
- » **Physical therapy**
- » **Social skills training**
- » **Tutoring**
- » **Counseling**
- » **Instructional aides such as daily organizers and communication tools**
- » **After school activities**
- » **Assistive technology**
- » **Transitional plans**
- » **Sex education**
- » **Vocational guidance and/or training**

Appropriate Expectations

Regulations may require specifying individual expectations and goals for each child's progress in the classroom.

- The expectations for children need to be based upon their cognitive functioning. For example, children who have cognitive impairments may become easily frustrated if the expectations are not understood or cannot be accomplished. If children cannot remember locations for materials because of a cognitive impairment, it will be difficult for them to put away their materials automatically.

- Classroom expectations need to be developmentally appropriate. For example, young children are not able to sit still for longer than 15 to 20 minutes.

- Expectations need to be understood by children. For example, a child may not understand what it means to be considerate. Using simple language such as "We will use kind words when we talk to others" may be easier for children to understand.

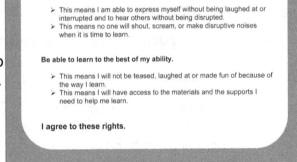

Post a Classroom Contract* in a prominent area of the classroom

- Classroom expectations need to be attainable, and feedback needs to be given to children to help them learn to monitor their progress. Children with special needs often have difficulties with immediate recall of information and with self-regulating their interactions in a group setting. Giving children feedback or acknowledgement provides guidance to them and supports their regulations and interactions.

Children need adult mediation to help them become active and engaged learners and to understand the purpose of learning.

---

* See Appendix "Classroom Rights"

Classroom Rights

Classroom Routines

Classroom Setting

Laws are designed to ensure that each child is safe and comfortable while being given appropriate learning instruction. Two important components of appropriate class settings are respect in the classroom and caring for the environment.

Respect:

- Children need to learn actions that are respectful of others in the classroom

- Children need to learn to accept others no matter what creed, color, disability, or learning difference there may be.

- Avoid having children grade each other's papers. This helps to lessen the anxiety and embarrassment some children may feel when they do not understand a task.

- Provide children with opportunities to discuss with the teacher privately questions or concerns they may have.

- A complaint box can help children anonymously express concerns.

Caring for the classroom:

- Give children a chore or job to help maintain the classroom. This helps them become invested in the room and learn to care for materials.

- Designate an area for children to post their work in the classroom. This also places a value on their work and encourages sharing.

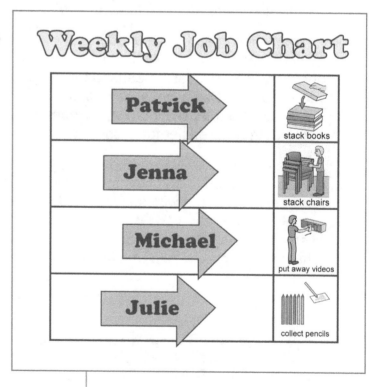

A "Weekly Job Chart" helps a child remember his or her chore.

Part II
Learning Strategies

Contents:

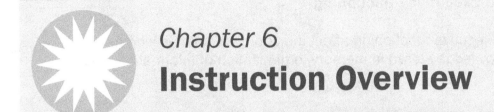

Chapter 6
Instruction Overview

Cognitive Effects

While the proper classroom environment is important in helping children with special needs learn, cognitive issues may require teachers to use more specialized learning strategies for specific subjects. These strategies are covered in Part 2.

The cognitive effects that impact learning are reflected in a variety of deficits. While some strategies in Part 2 overlap techniques discussed in Part 1, they are expanded where appropriate for specific topics.

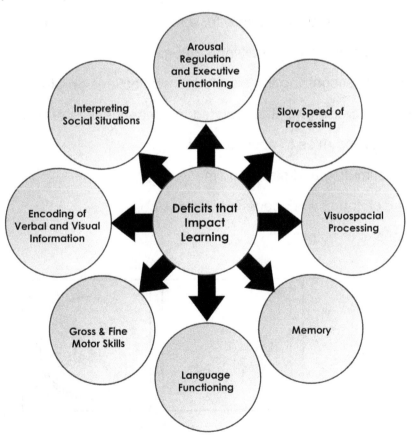

Instruction Overview
Cognitive Effects

Arousal Regulation and Executive Functioning

Arousal regulation and executive functioning affect the coordination of linking new information with prior knowledge stored in memory, organization of information, and planning responses.

Poor executive functioning can make it difficult to initiate and stop actions, monitor and change behavior as needed, anticipate outcomes, handle novel tasks, and think abstractly. These deficits can interfere with the individual's ability to regulate and, as children enter late childhood or early adolescent, to evaluate their own behavior and academic performance.

▶▶▶**How difficulties with executive functioning may be exhibited:**

- Inconsistent ability to modulate behavior in regards to the environment

  Example: continues to be highly active when returning to the classroom from the playground.

- Difficulties adjusting vocal intonation and volume

- Problems when required to prepare for a new activity or challenge

- Limited skills to shift problem solving strategies

- Weaknesses in recognizing the effects of one's actions on others

- Unaware of the cause and effect related to consequences and past actions

- Difficulties applying rules to novel situations

- Difficulties estimating and planning time

- Difficulties monitoring work pace in the classroom

- Slow responses or output

Slow Speed of Processing

Processing speed refers to the recognition of information and the ability to respond.

▶▶▶ **How difficulties with speed of processing may be exhibited:**

- Difficulties understanding and responding to verbal directions

- Difficulties following the thread of conversations

- Weaknesses recognizing and responding to verbal and visual cues, especially if they are presented quickly

- Slow responses or output

Visuospatial Processing

Skills that require the recognition of patterns, the distinguishing of shapes, the need to mentally manipulate shapes to solve problems, and the skills to determine the distances and locations of items or people present difficulties for children with visual spatial deficits.

▶▶▶ **How visuospatial deficits may be exhibited:**

- Problems with mathematics

- Difficulties locating sentences embedded in a passage when reading

- Difficulties using a separate answer sheet during a test

- Difficulties copying from the board

- Difficulties judging distance

- Difficulties understanding the layout of a room or environment

- Difficulties reading maps or directions

Give your student a short paragraph to read and have him or her find a particular word in the paragraph.

Today was Carla's birthday. She was very excited and got up early. No one was awake yet, not even their dog Pookie! Very quietly, she crept downstairs. On the stairs, she stepped on her sister's toy elephant and it made a loud "woo-woo" noise! She paused, certain that her mother had heard and would come downstairs to see what the ruckus was about.

Instruction Overview
Cognitive Effects

Memory

Children with special needs may exhibit difficulties with operations required to process, store, and retrieve information from the memory system.

These children often have difficulties simultaneously processing multiple sources of information. Due to difficulties with intake, information may not be stored effectively in long term memory for future use. Since memory is an integrated system that utilizes a multitude of senses to gather new data, process the information to create ideas, and store the relevant information for future use, these problems may impede the student's ability to learn across many subjects.

▶▶▶**How difficulties with memory may be exhibited:**

- Difficulties retaining new information

- Limited use of semantic and spatial association to help with storage

- Inconsistent locating and retrieving prior knowledge

- Inability to connect new information to prior knowledge to form new concepts

Language Functioning

Language functioning entails the ability to comprehend oral and written language, to use words to communicate ideas, and to converse effectively and fluently.

Significant language differences exist across different special needs groups. For example, children with Fetal Alcohol Spectrum Disorders may exhibit relative strength in their ability to speak fluently while poor communication skill is one of the markers for autism. Within disorders language functionality can also vary greatly. Children with low functioning autism may be nonverbal while children with high functioning autism may be fluent. Even if a child with special needs can state their needs and retell events, they often do not understand the underlying meanings conveyed during exchanges. The inability to understand information presented by others can be misleading given a child's skills to generate comments and verbalize their wants.

▶▶▶ How difficulties with language functioning may be exhibited:

- Inability to infer the underlying messages during interpersonal exchanges

- Difficulties maintaining and following the topic of conversation

- Difficulties with social discourse and pragmatics

- Difficulties using verbal mediation as a problem solving technique

- Problems comprehending written language, especially when required to infer information

- Difficulties using written language to express ideas

Written language requires the use of other skills that often are impacted by special needs. To convey messages through writing, children need to utilize graphomotor skills (handwriting), as well as organize the information, plan the format of the piece, maintain the thread of the topic, and apply grammar and style rules to complete the task.

Instruction Overview

Cognitive Effects

Gross and Fine Motor Skills

Motor function can be separated into gross and fine motor skills.

▶▶▶**How difficulties with gross motor skills may be exhibited:**

- Poor muscle tone, grasp, and other movements

- Difficulties participating in physical activities, such as running or riding a bike

- Difficulties using tools or utensils

- Clumsiness

▶▶▶**How difficulties with fine motor skills may be exhibited:**

- Weak hand-eye coordination

- Problems doing tasks that require the hand for guided intake

- Difficulties doing crafts, coloring, and using scissors

- Difficulties writing

- Difficulties with sports

Lined Writing and "Stop-N-Go" paper are good tools for practicing writing skills.*

Encoding of Verbal and Visual Information

Encoding of verbal and visual information refers to the registration of information for additional processing and/or storage in the memory system.

▶▶▶**How difficulties with encoding verbal and visual information may be exhibited:**

- Limited retention of quickly presented information

- Require frequent and longer exposure durations of stimuli

*Repeating information using both sound and visuals may be needed when learning new skills, such as crossing a street as shown in this Do2Learn safety song.***

---

* See Appendix "Stop-N-Go Paper" and "Lined Writing Paper"
** Available at www.Do2Learn.com

Examples of activities to improve motor skills include Mazes, Cut-N-Paste, and Dauber/Sticker Activities.*

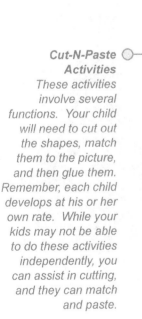

Maze Activities
Have your child draw a line from the starting picture to the ending picture. Focus on staying inside the lines of the maze. Try using colored pencils, highlighters, crayons, or even paint. Using different materials offers a variety of sensory input. Introducing new materials as you work also makes tasks more interesting and fun for children to complete.

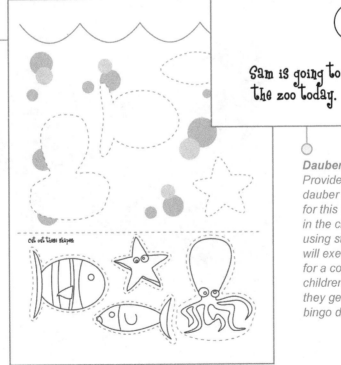

Cut-N-Paste Activities
These activities involve several functions. Your child will need to cut out the shapes, match them to the picture, and then glue them. Remember, each child develops at his or her own rate. While your kids may not be able to do these activities independently, you can assist in cutting, and they can match and paste.

Dauber/Sticker Activities
Provide your child with a bingo dauber or large round stickers for this activity. Let your child fill in the circles accordingly. While using stickers for these activities will exercise the muscles needed for a correct pincer grasp, many children enjoy the sensory input they get from stamping with the bingo dauber.

* Examples from the "Fine Motor Skills Activity Book", available at www.Do2Learn.com

Instruction Overview
Cognitive Effects

Interpreting Social Situations

Children with special needs may exhibit difficulties with interpreting social situations and group dynamics. Due to possible difficulties in language, self-regulation and monitoring, and memory, children may experience difficulties remembering and learning from previous experiences, maintaining the topic of discussion, easily shifting and modulating reactions to peers, attending to the visual information presented during social discourse, and interpreting the nonverbal cues and body language.

▶▶▶**How difficulties with interpreting social situations may be exhibited:**

- Disconnected comments

- Misunderstanding of nonverbal cues and facial expressions

- Confusion interpreting vocal inflections

- Inability to predict the effects of actions on others

- Lack of awareness of the messages conveyed through gesture

- Literal interpretation of language - such as missing the humor in jokes and misinterpreting sarcasm

- Difficulties with spatial information and social boundaries

- Difficulties with arousal regulation and modulating effect as the scenario or setting changes

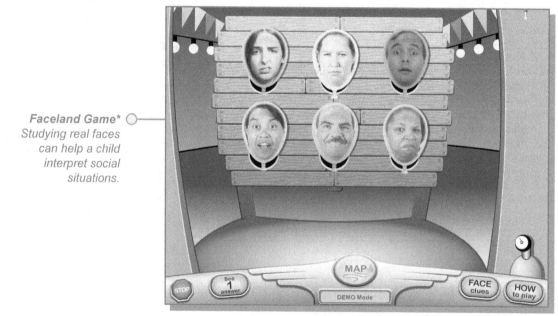

Faceland Game* Studying real faces can help a child interpret social situations.

Instruction Overview
Cognitive Effects

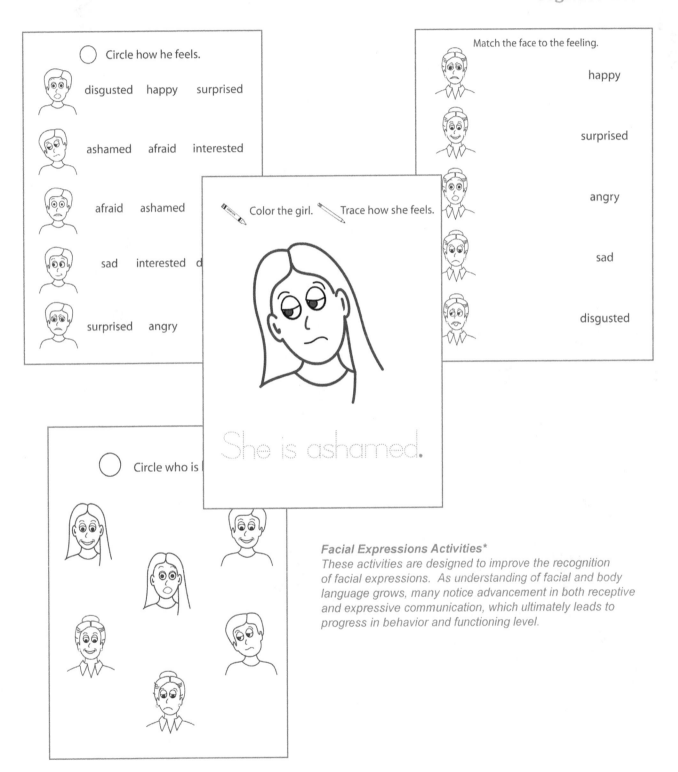

Circle how he feels.

disgusted   happy   surprised

ashamed   afraid   interested

afraid   ashamed

sad   interested   d

surprised   angry

Match the face to the feeling.

happy

surprised

angry

sad

disgusted

Color the girl.   Trace how she feels.

She is ashamed.

Circle who is

Facial Expressions Activities*
*These activities are designed to improve the recognition
of facial expressions. As understanding of facial and body
language grows, many notice advancement in both receptive
and expressive communication, which ultimately leads to
progress in behavior and functioning level.*

* Examples from the "Feelings & Emotions Workbook", available at www.Do2Learn.com

Chapter 7
Problem Solving

Problem solving and thinking skills can be taught to children with special needs to help them compensate for inherent difficulties. It is important that children be given direct instruction on the use of these skills within their curriculum.

Given the secondary disabilities caused by special needs, children with special needs benefit from explicit instruction that includes:

- How to select the appropriate problem solving skill.

- How to gather the necessary information.

- How to apply the skill to solve a problem.

- How to shift problem-solving strategies when the original strategy is ineffective.

- How to use the skills across academic domains and life situations.

Specific problem solving approaches depend on the task children need to solve. However, there are general thinking strategies to help children learn efficiently in the classroom.

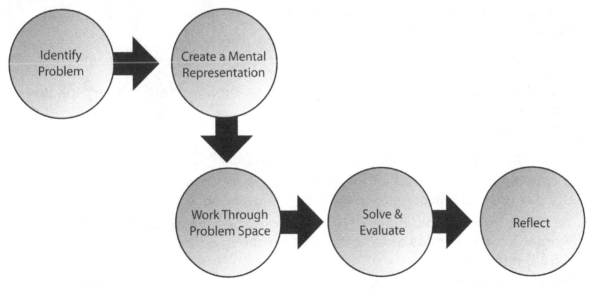

Identify Problem

It is important for the student to recognize what the problem is in order to begin to solve it. They need to be able to focus on the presentation as well as gather all the information needed.

FOCUSING

» **Direct the student to the problem by using statements such as "Look here." Color code important information written on an overhead board.**

» **Present the specific purpose of the task or assignment to the student. Use rubrics to define the expectations.**

DATA GATHERING

Teach children to use self-questioning techniques:

» *What do you already know?*

» *What looks familiar?*

» *What do you need to do?*

» *What are the features of the task?*

» *What is important?*

SELECTION OF RELEVANT INFORMATION

» **Teach children to recognize and highlight words in problems that indicate a procedure.**

» **Use guided questions to direct selection of information. This will direct the student to focus on the plot of the story.**

  For example: *When reading, do you think this story could really happen?*

» **Use study guides to help direct children to select important information during lectures.**

SEEKING CLARIFICATION

» **If children have gathered information and cannot determine what they need to do, cue them to ask questions for more information.**

» **To check for understanding, have children restate the directions in their own words; if they state the directions back verbatim, encourage them to use different words.**

» **Provide children with any clarification to help understand the problem.**

Create a Mental Representation

Once the problem is identified, a mental representation needs to be created to show the problem that needs solving.

CONNECT TO PRIOR KNOWLEDGE

» **Use scripted analogies and examples. "If I know… then I know…"**
» **Complete a brainstorming exercise to cue children to access prior knowledge.**
» **Keep informative texts related to the topic visible around the classroom as a visual reminder.**

VISUALIZING

» **Have children learn to create mental imagery.**
» **Have children orally describe characters or objects related to a subject.**
» **Direct children to use specific descriptive words as they tell about an item. For example, have them indicate the pattern on a ball they are describing.**
» **Have children use gestures to indicate size, movement, or location and have them reference to themselves. Use prompts such as, "Is the boy shorter or taller than you?" to encourage them to gesture. Gesturing will give insight into their perspectives and views.**

PICTORIAL

Have children draw simple number lines, tally marks, and other diagrams to represent numbers, groups, or objects. Teach them to make charts of the data.

Pictorial Diagram

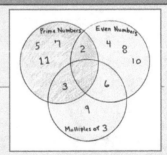

SYMBOLIC

Have children create signs or use symbols to represent their problem.

For example: "Tom is taller than Bob can be shown as: T > B therefore B < T."

Problem Solving
Create a Mental Representation

DEMONSTRATIVE

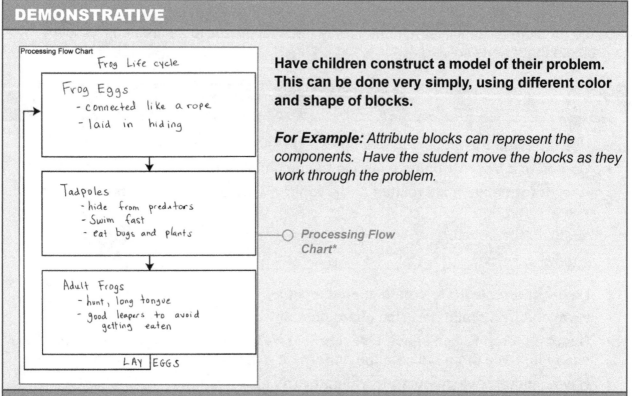

Have children construct a model of their problem. This can be done very simply, using different color and shape of blocks.

For Example: Attribute blocks can represent the components. Have the student move the blocks as they work through the problem.

○ Processing Flow Chart*

COMPARE, CONTRAST, CATEGORIZE

Use Semantic Feature Analysis* or other exercises that help children look at the similarities and differences.

Semantic Feature Analysis* ○

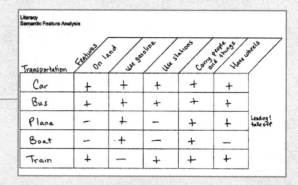

PREDICTION

Have children tell, write, or draw their predictions of the outcome before completing the task or assignment.

Work Through Problem Space

The mental representations help to maintain the background information and the elements needed to solve the problem. Children are required to select the most appropriate strategy to determine the solution. General thinking skills are necessary while problem solving strategies are often task specific.

DETERMINING THE STRATEGY

» **Teach children to look for keywords to guide their problem solving. For example, keep a chart on their desk of common words used to indicate a math procedure.**

» **Teach children to recognize the purpose of the problem. For example, have the students ask themselves, "Can I find a definite answer?"**

» **Have children reword the problem in their own words.**

» **Have children create checklists or diagrams showing the steps to the problem and list their evidence in order of relevance.**

» **Direct children to create an argument or a defense if they are working with opinions, judgments, and claims. Have children write or show their predicted outcomes.**

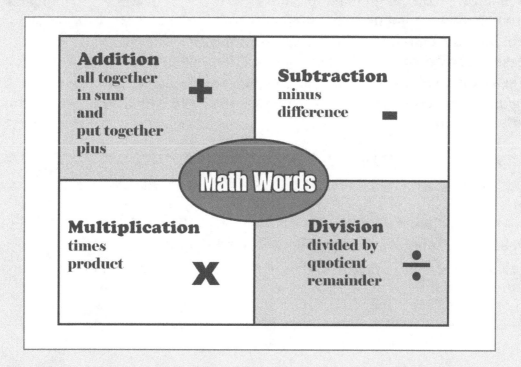

Problem Solving

Work Through Problem Space

ADJUSTING/SHIFTING THE STRATEGY

» Engage the students in a discussion about their method of solving the problem and have them tell why they chose that strategy.

» If a strategy isn't successful, have the children circle or mark the area where they are stuck. Direct them to work backwards through the problem.

» Have children highlight the keywords in the problem to see if they understood correctly the procedure or purpose.

» Encourage children not to erase when they make a mistake. Have them circle the error and write the correct answer next to the error. Go back and work through the problem to see where the breakdown occurred.

» Direct children to use self-questions such as "What if…?" to change the approach to the problem and to change their perspective.

» Encourage children to talk with others in the class. At times, others may see things differently and help with a solution.

» Make a pro and con list and select the next most viable option to use to solve the problem. Have children provide reasons as to why they support trying the different method.

RESTRUCTURING MENTAL SPACE

» After clarifying the information, direct children to adjust their representation.

» Make lists of choices to show alternative strategies.

» Use a color-coding system, highlight changes when adjusting the representation.

Solve and Evaluate

Children need to find the solution, to check the solution's accuracy, and adjust the problem solving technique if needed.

REPRESENTATION OF SOLUTION

» Make sure the expression of the solution is a clear match with the outcome goal or purpose of the problem. For example, a solution to an equation or word problem in math needs to be written as an equation and reflect the central elements used to solve it.

» Make sure children use terminology that they normally use to ensure they are able to understand and explain their solutions.

» Use a variety of thinking words to explain the solution – Use specific words that tell about the process.

Examples:
When giving a solution to a math problem use words like "answer".
When telling about a summary from an author's opinion use words like "claim" or "believe".

» Post a list of thinking words and color code according to the type of thoughts they tell.

> **Words for Thinking**
>
> Infer
> Inspect
> Inquire
> Grasp
> Understand   Verify   Deliberate
> Define   Propose
> Identify
> Investigate   Recognize
> Question
> Glean   Deduce
> Theorize
> Study   Analyze

EVALUATE

» Discuss the procedures used to solve the problem.

» Have children grade themselves. Have children circle an answer or word they wrote that they thought was clearly written or select a piece of work they felt they learned well and have them tell why.

VERIFY

» Depending on the type of problem, compare with the student different possible solutions to the problem. Discuss with the student how someone else determined the answer and what was similar and different about their problem solving technique.

» Have children grade an additional problem finding the same answer in a different way. Have them compare the two methods. Make sure the other problem was not completed by a student in the class.

Problem Solving
Reflect

Reflect

After the process is completed, the student will need to evaluate the effectiveness of the strategies and the thinking processes. The reflection process helps children register the strategies in memory for future use.

REVIEW

» **Take time once the process is completed to review what was learned with the children. This can be done through discussion.**

» **Give a novel task where the student must use the same problem solving techniques to assess understanding.**

» **Encourage children to make a list of new questions they thought of after solving the problem. Use the questions to guide additional exploration into a topic or area.**

» **Ask children to create a problem and solve it by using the technique.**

TRANSFER

» **Provide many opportunities across academic subjects for children to use the strategies.**

» **Directly relate the ideas to things that happen every day.**

» **Respond to children's use of strategies in other settings. Specifically point out the strategy use. This will encourage children to continue to use similar techniques to solve problems in that context.**

For Example: If a student compared a familiar word to an unknown word in order to read the word, say to the student, "Great, you used something you already knew to figure out the new word."

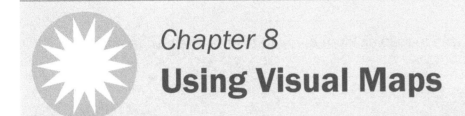

Chapter 8
Using Visual Maps

The purpose of using visual mapping techniques is to help children generate, organize, and expand their thoughts. Maps provide a visual representation of their thought processes. Mapping exercises can be used across academic subjects and used with a variety of age groups.

When using visual maps, it is important to:

1. Help children determine the type of thinking they need to do to solve a problem and teach them to select an appropriate tool to demonstrate their thinking. For example, if they are beginning to research a topic, it may be beneficial for a student to construct a brainstorming bubble. This may assist to structure their thinking on a topic and to connect to prior knowledge.

2. Gradually introduce mapping techniques, starting with one type of map at a time. Once children feel comfortable using a type of map across subjects, then introduce a new kind. Gradually increase usage and complexity.

3. At first, children may need to be given a sheet showing the structure of the type of map and may begin to use the mapping technique by filling in the circles or frame. But, since the purpose of the visual maps is to help children generate and organize their thoughts, it is important to use the original frame minimally and encourage children to create visual maps independently to visually demonstrate their thinking.

4. Not all children use the same types of maps well. Encourage children to use the type of mapping technique that they are comfortable using and that supports their learning.

5. Provide children with many opportunities to transfer their information to solve a variety of problems.

After children have mastered the concept of visual maps, have them make their own forms from scratch .

Using Visual Maps
Brainstorming Maps

Brainstorming Maps*

Brainstorming maps can be used to help children connect to prior knowledge and to generate ideas about a topic.

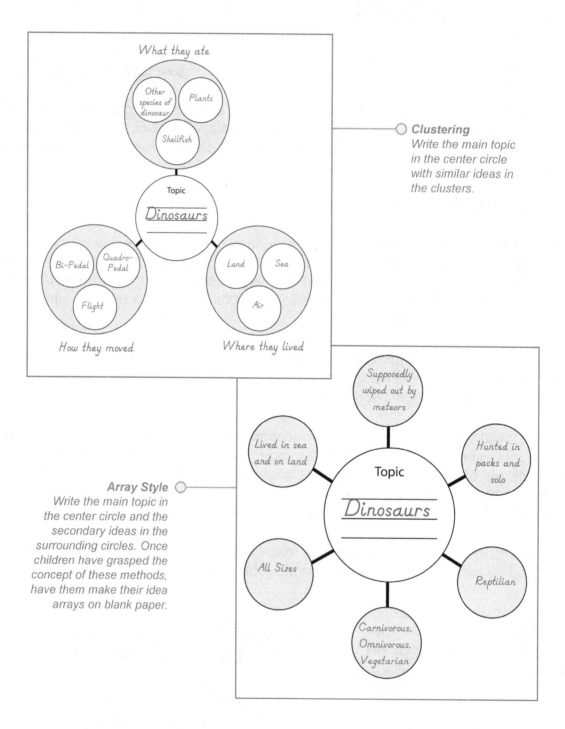

Clustering
Write the main topic in the center circle with similar ideas in the clusters.

Array Style
Write the main topic in the center circle and the secondary ideas in the surrounding circles. Once children have grasped the concept of these methods, have them make their idea arrays on blank paper.

Organizing Maps*

Organizing maps guide children to classify and to think about the relevance and order of the information depending on a topic or class.

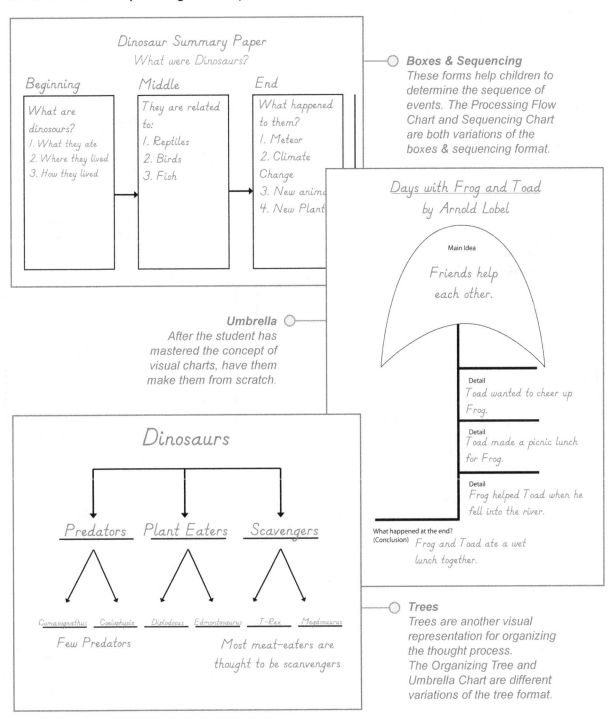

Boxes & Sequencing
These forms help children to determine the sequence of events. The Processing Flow Chart and Sequencing Chart are both variations of the boxes & sequencing format.

Umbrella
After the student has mastered the concept of visual charts, have them make them from scratch.

Trees
Trees are another visual representation for organizing the thought process. The Organizing Tree and Umbrella Chart are different variations of the tree format.

* See Appendix "Organizing Maps"

Using Visual Maps
Processing Maps

Processing Maps*

Processing maps help children to think how related topics or pieces of information interact with each other and help them think about the possible outcomes.

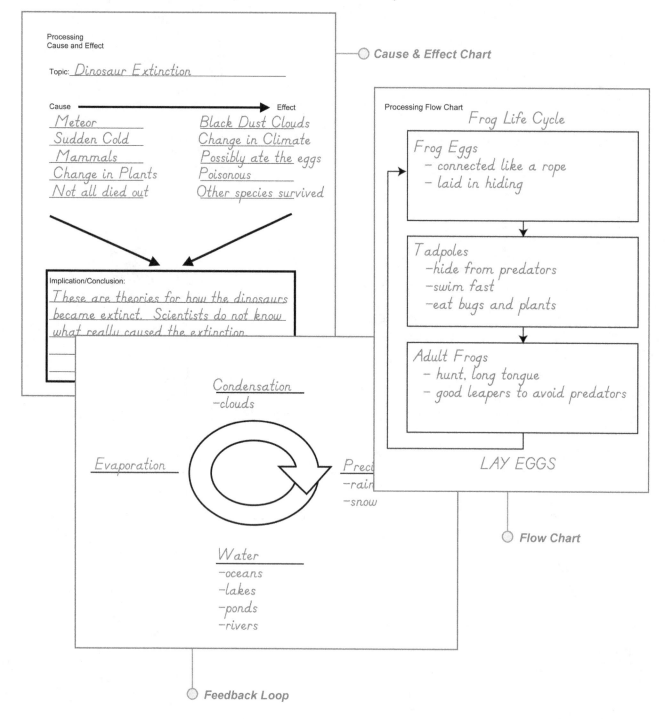

Processing
Cause and Effect

Topic: *Dinosaur Extinction*

Cause ⟶ Effect

Meteor	*Black Dust Clouds*
Sudden Cold	*Change in Climate*
Mammals	*Possibly ate the eggs*
Change in Plants	*Poisonous*
Not all died out	*Other species survived*

Implication/Conclusion:
These are theories for how the dinosaurs became extinct. Scientists do not know what really caused the extinction.

○ **Cause & Effect Chart**

Processing Flow Chart

Frog Life Cycle

Frog Eggs
 - connected like a rope
 - laid in hiding

Tadpoles
 -hide from predators
 -swim fast
 -eat bugs and plants

Adult Frogs
 - hunt, long tongue
 - good leapers to avoid predators

LAY EGGS

○ **Flow Chart**

Condensation
-clouds

Evaporation

Preci
-rain
-snow

Water
-oceans
-lakes
-ponds
-rivers

○ **Feedback Loop**

Chapter 9
Reading

In order to become efficient readers, children need to be able to perceive and manipulate the sounds in words, connect the sounds to the letter or letter patterns, read the words quickly, and link meaning to the text. Difficulties in one or more of these areas can hinder children's progress when learning to read. Effective reading programs incorporate direct instruction in the areas of sound awareness, word attack or decoding, fluency, and reading comprehension.

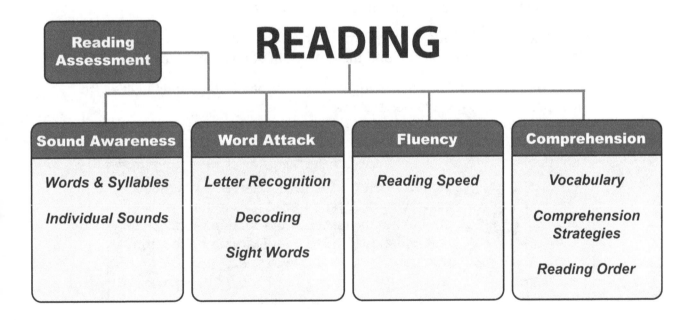

84   **Learning Strategies**

Reading

Reading Assessment

Reading Assessment

Efficient reading requires children to understand the relationship between the sounds and the letters, maintain an adequate sight word base knowledge, understand the structure of language, and synthesize these skills. The purpose of reading is to gather information from the text. Children need to link words to their meaning and apply words to a context that makes sense to become efficient readers.

Difficulties in one or more of the areas can impact children's progress in learning to read. It is important to assess children's reading progress accurately in order to devise appropriate instructional methods and strategies to support children in this process.

To assess reading, consider:

- The children's ages and developmental profiles

- Do children have any sensory impairment that could impact learning to read?

- The children's language functioning, including vocabulary knowledge, comprehension, and recognition of sound boundaries in words

- Formulating a specific question regarding children's difficulty in reading, such as do children recognize and blend the individual sounds in words?

- The purpose of the reading assessment (e.g. to detect reading difficulties, to monitor progress, to assess general reading skills)

Some children who have received a diagnosis of specific reading disability will require a structured, systematic approach to reading instruction tailored to their learning profile from a reading and/or language specialist.

Sound Awareness
Words & Syllables

The awareness and the skills to recognize and to manipulate the sounds in spoken words are important elements in the early elementary level when learning to read. This is called phonological awareness.

Young children who are not aware of the individual sounds in spoken words often exhibit difficulties linking the sounds to the print to decode words using phonics when they begin to read. With direct instruction, children can learn to analyze the sounds within spoken words.

Training of sound awareness needs to begin with words in sentences and with syllables. This introduces the sound boundaries of words.

WORDS & SYLLABLES ACTIVITIES

» **Count the words heard in sentence. Have the children use different colored blocks, chips, or pieces of felt to show how many words they hear.**

» **Practice counting the syllables heard in a word. Say words and have children clap or snap the number of syllables they hear in words.**

» **Play "Which word is longer?" Present children with two words, said one at a time without a visual. Ask children to repeat the words and then have them tell which word sounds longer.**

basketball

zoo

» **Play rhyming games, such as "I spy a word that rhymes with 'top.'" Have children generate words or find other words in the classroom that rhyme with top.**

» **Read poetry together.**

» **Tell familiar rhymes or stories, but change the words or leave out words and see if children can replace the missing words.**

Reading

Sound Awareness

Individual Sounds

Once children have mastered working with word discrimination and with the sound chunks (syllables) in words, begin working with the individual sounds in words. Start with having the children focus on the initial sounds in words, then work on the ending sounds. After children have grasped the beginning and ending sounds in words, work with manipulating the medial sounds.

INDIVIDUAL SOUNDS IN WORDS

» **Play sound discrimination games. Say two words and see if they can tell if the words begin with the same sound or with a different sound. Gradually increase the number of words presented to children, where there may be two words with the same beginning sound and a foil. Have children tell the word that begins with the different sound. This format can be used when working with ending and medial sounds in words.**

» **Have children generate chains of words that use a targeted beginning or ending sound.**

» **Use picture cards and have children sort the pictures according to the targeted sound. When working with more than one sound, especially at the beginning, start with sounds that are not closely related and gradually move to closely related sounds as children become proficient at distinguishing sounds.**

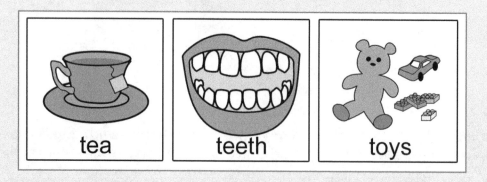

INDIVIDUAL SOUNDS IN WORDS

» Have children use colored blocks, chips, or felts to represent each sound they hear in a word. Touch each chip and say the sounds slowly. Slide the chips together and have children pronounce the word. Create a Separate Sounds Activity to play with children.

Separate Sounds Activity

Setup:

» *Place a picture card showing a simple word on a mat. Be sure to use words that start with consonants.*

» *Give your student a pile of multi-colored chips or checkers.*

Play:
Pick one colored chip for each sound in the word and place it below. For example, the word "big" has three distinct sounds- "b" + "i" + "g", so the student will select a different colored chip for each sound and place it below.

Variations:
Select a word that repeats one of the consonants. For example, the word "mom" has only two distinct sounds "m" + "o" + "m", so the student will use the same color chip for both "m" sounds.

Reading

Sound Awareness

INDIVIDUAL SOUNDS IN WORDS

» Have children tap the number of sounds they hear in a word on their fingers and blend the sounds to pronounce the word. After children separate the sounds, it is important to have them say the word normally to associate the sound pieces to the whole word.

» Isolate the sounds in the words and have children blend the sounds to pronounce the word – for example say /s/.../a/.../t/ and have the children blend the sounds and say the word "sat". Practice with substituting sounds in words. For example, say the word "cat" and have children substitute the /c/ in "cat" with an /s/ to make "sat". This activity can be done with beginning, medial, and ending sounds in words.

» Play Pig Latin games – Change children's names by adding common endings such as adding /ious/ to the end of Jane to make the name Janious. Children find this activity amusing and will begin to add endings to change words to other objects and words.

» Sound bingos are useful whole class activities to support awareness of sounds in words. There are many commercial bingo games available at most local school supply stores.

Sound Bingo
Setup:

» *Game board laid out on a 5x5 grid containing Picture cards of simple images.*

» *Chips or Checkers*

Play:
Each player has his or her own board.

Tell each player to cover up all the pictures on his or her board that start or end with a particular sound. For example, say "Cover up all the pictures that begin with a 'c' sound," or "Cover up all the pictures that end in a 'b' sound."

Use consonants, not vowels, for kids at this level of learning.

When a player gets 5 chips in a row (horizontally, vertically, or diagonally), he or she calls out "Bingo!" and wins the round.

Word Attack
Letter Recognition

Efficient letter recognition is a necessary early literacy skill. Research has indicated that young children who demonstrate difficulties with letter recognition often struggle to learn to read as they progress in school. Young children need to develop the insight that sounds are represented by a letter or by letter combinations in text.

LETTER RECOGNITION

» When introducing letters, begin with the most common. Try to sequence introduction of letters or patterns that do not look alike or sound similar to avoid confusion. For example, do not introduce /f/ and /th/ together.

» Play matching games and concentration games to match letters and combinations.

» Have children sort words that begin or end with a particular letter. This will help children learn to scan the word and categorize words according to a rule.

» Have a letter of the week and encourage children to locate words that have that beginning or ending letter. Have letter "show and tell" where children bring in an object that they have found that begins with a targeted letter.

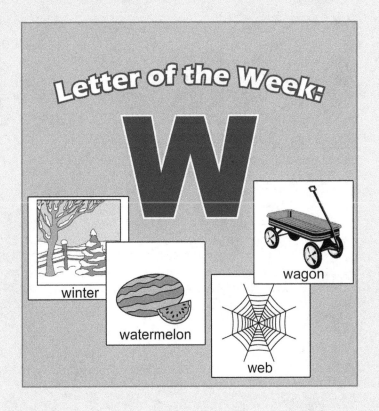

Reading

Word Attack

LETTER RECOGNITION

» **Play Go Fish for Letters.**

Go Fish For Letters*

Setup:

» *Create picture cards with letters of the alphabet and pictures cut into playing cards. Make the cards larger and more durable by gluing each alphabet card to an index card.*

» *Each player is dealt 6 cards, and the remaining cards are placed face down in a pile.*

To Play:
Play is exactly like traditional Go Fish, except instead of matching numbers, players match the sounds of each letter, not the name. For older children, use cards that only have letters on them and no pictures.

Other variations :
Play Memory with the alphabet cards. Cards are laid out in a grid face down, and players take turns flipping pairs of cards over. On each turn, the player will first turn one card over, then a second. If the two cards match, the player scores one point, the two cards are removed from the game, and the player gets another turn. If they do not match, the cards are turned back over. The object is to match more pairs of cards than the opposing player.

Make a Matching folder activity with the cards. Glue one of each letter to the inside of a file folder. Have your student match the remaining letters to those glued on the folder. Make this a more durable activity by laminating the folder and using Velcro to affix pairs together.

Decoding

Decoding refers to children's ability to link the sounds to the letter or letter patterns to decipher unknown words. As children become proficient with recognizing letters and associating their sounds to letters, then activities that focus on word building can be implemented.

DECODING

» **To help notice similarities and differences among words, have children write as many words that contain a word family as they can. After they generate words, have them read the words, circle the differences among the words and underline the patterns of words in their list. This will help children to recognize onsets and rhymes.**

» **Incorporate writing activities to provide opportunities for children to link sound to print and words to meaning.**

» **Play games like hangman to teach specific word strategies and generalizations. For example, when selecting letters, point out that every word must have a vowel. Games like hangman provide opportunities to work with spelling and the general guidelines of word structure.**

» **Play <u>Scrabble, Jr</u>. or <u>Scrabble</u>. This will encourage children to think and to generate words as well as provide spelling practice.**

» **Teach children specific strategies to decode words. Have children use scripted analogies or key words to identify patterns that can be used in recognizing other words that contain the same pattern.**

» **Direct children to locate smaller words within larger words.**

» **Have children learn to recognize common endings such as –ing and -ed and separate the endings from the root or base word.**

Reading
Word Attack

Sight Words

To support efficient reading, children need to be able to recognize some common words automatically. These words occur frequently in text.

SIGHT WORDS

Using the Dolch word list or the Fry word list, make two sets of flash cards for each word. Gradually expand the card deck as the student learns new words. Many games to practice with sight words can be played with these decks and include:

» **"Go Fish with Sight Words."**

» **"Sight Word Rummy" where children make books of sight words that begin with the same letter.**

» **"Sight Word Snap." This game requires children to put down a card at the same time. If the word is the same on the cards, a player snaps his or her fingers (or says 'snap') and reads the word on the card. This becomes their match. If the words do not match, the cards get placed in a pool. Play continues, and the players can match the cards that are put down or match their words to the words in the pool. The game is completed once all words are paired.**

» **"Sight Word Memory."**

» **"Sight Word Bingo." There are many commercially produced "Sight Word Bingo" games on the market.**

Fluency
Reading Speed

To be fluent readers, children need to develop efficient word attack and have an adequate sight word base. Some children struggle to synthesize the skills required to read at an appropriate pace. They may be able to decode words when reading lists or words in isolation but struggle with reading text. This interferes with reading comprehension. It is important that children develop the efficient decoding skills needed to read fluently.

ACTIVITIES TO SUPPORT READING FLUENCY

» **Provide opportunities for repeated readings. Have children re-read short sections or stories to practice with pacing. Select a book below the student's independent reading level. This will remove the child's need to process and to decode new words and will direct his or her focus to the rhythm of the speech. Have children read using different tones and pitches to vary the exercise and to explore how mood relates to the voice.**

» **Have children verbally chase the instructor as they read. First the teacher reads the section out loud while the students listen. Then the students read the section out loud while the teacher listens. Finally, the teacher reads and children verbally chase the teacher reading. The teacher needs to set the pacing. Typically, children will remain one or two words behind the teacher. After the teacher and children finish, the students read the section orally again. Discuss with children how their reading sounded after they practiced reading with the instructor.**

» **Provide time in the classroom for children to explore a variety of books. When helping a student to select a book for independent reading, have the student read a page out loud from the book. If the student makes five or more reading errors, then the book is too difficult. Guide the student to make another selection.**

» **Timed readings at an independent reading level can be used to help track a child's reading fluency. Fluent readers by the age of 12 need to have a read rate of greater than 100 words per minute when reading at their independent level.**

Reading
Comprehension

Comprehension
Vocabulary

Research has suggested that the more encounters children have with word meanings, the more vocabulary they can acquire. Instruction to support vocabulary development needs to be included in the reading instruction.

VOCABULARY

» **Read out loud to the class. Reading out loud provides exposure to new words and opportunities for children to ask and discuss word meanings.**

» **When working with a topic or related words, use semantic mappings to help children compare and contrast words. This will help them to generate relationships and encourage them to draw conclusions about the relationships and meanings.**

» **Have children make word webs to explore the features and meanings of words.**

» **Teach children to visualize the meanings of words. For example, encourage children to create a mental picture and to process the elements of the object or word. This may encourage them to think more about meanings and contexts.**

» **Establish an independent reading time in the classroom. During this time, sit with children and encourage them to discuss the story and any words they have come across that they find interesting.**

» **Teach children to categorize words. This will help generate context that creates a foundation to support understanding and links to other words.**

» **Create a classroom dictionary of new words learned. Place a notebook in a central location. Separate the notebook into categories. Try to relate the dictionary to themes studied in the classroom. Some category headings may include: animals, rocks and minerals, transportation, man made objects. Use student generated dictionaries as reference sources for children.**

Comprehension Strategies

Often children struggle to recognize important elements of text, summarize, and synthesize the information to create new knowledge. To make sure children understand what they are reading, they need to be able to put the text in their own words, prioritize the information, and draw conclusions from the salient information. Reading instruction needs to include strategies to support the children's understanding of text.

COMPREHENSION STRATEGIES

» Use open-ended, guiding questions to help children think about a text as they read and to focus on important information. Have children complete a reading response after they read a passage or a story to help connect the information.

» Teach children to summarize the story in their own words. This will help children focus on the meaning of the text. Use concept maps to help children show the sequence of the story and to maintain the primary elements.

» Direct children to locate repetitive information found in the text. Use visuals to help children locate the main characters and actions. For example, using different colored blocks or different shapes, have children select a shape to represent the characters in the story. After the children read the story, have the them place the blocks as they retell the story. Direct them to notice which block occurs most frequently in each scene of their retelling. Discuss with them why this character would probably be the main character.

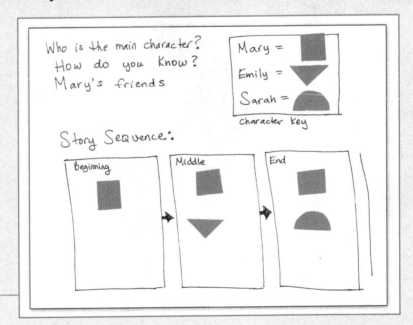

Idea Blocks for Reading

Reading

Comprehension

COMPREHENSION STRATEGIES

» Teach children to recognize the structure of texts. For example, informational texts typically use a topic statement, followed by supporting details, and ending with a conclusion. Recognizing the structure of text can help children locate pertinent information. Also, recognizing the story structure in fiction, such as the plot structure, can help children learn to make inferences about relationships among characters in the story.

» Guide children to become aware of their reading process. Using self-questioning can help them learn to make analogies to compare sources of information and help them to monitor their understanding. Teach children to generate and answer their own questions as they read.

For example: Children can learn to ask themselves, "What am I reading about and why," to guide them to focus on the relevant information.

Reading Order

Many children have difficulty understanding how to read or search for information on a page. This is an important skill for both math and reading.

Both read and search order:

- **Start from the left and read to the right side on each line.**

- **Move down the page one line at a time from page top to page bottom, reading each line left to right.**

When first learning, visually cue children where to look by pointing to the appropriate place and speaking. You may cover parts of the page to direct the children's attention to the correct section. Start with Reading Order and progress to Searching Order after children understand the correct pattern.

READING ORDER VISUAL PRACTICE

Start with a simple page with separate pictures.
1. **Cover all but the first line with a blank sheet and read the images from left to right, using your finger to show the order.**
2. **Say each image as you point to it. Have the child follow along with his/her finger.**
3. **Move the blank sheet down the page, uncovering one line at a time and reading that line from left to right until all images on the page are read.**
4. **When the child is ready, let him/her point to and say each image from left to right as you move the blank sheet down the page.**
5. **As the final lesson, repeat the actions of reading and pointing to each image on the page from top to bottom, left to right, without using the blank sheet. You may need to do this first with the child following as you point and say each image name.**

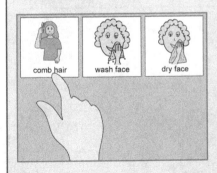  

SEARCHING ORDER VISUAL PRACTICE

1. Start with a simple page with separate 2" pictures.

2. Make two copies of the page in two different colors. Laminate or cover pages with clear contact paper. Cut one page into separate images.

3. Pick one image from the cut up page and place it at the top of the page to search.

4. Cover all but the first line with a blank sheet and read the images from left to right, using your finger to show the order.

5. Say the image as you point to it. Have the child follow along with his/her finger.

6. Compare each image as you point to it with the one you are searching for, shown above the page. If it matches, place the cut out image over the identical image on the page and stop the search.

7. Pick another image and repeat the search until all images on the page are covered with the identical image in the different color.

8. When the child is ready, let him/her search the page line-by-line for the matching image as you move the blank sheet down the page. Repeat until all images on the page are replaced by the new colored copies.

9. As the final lesson, repeat the search pattern of reading and pointing to each image while searching for the match without using the blank sheet. You may need to do this first with the child following.

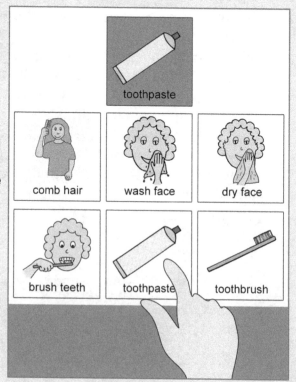

SEARCHING ORDER VISUAL PRACTICE

Variations for Read and Search:

1. **Use a page of 1-inch images for more difficulty.**
2. **Use more fun pages from books such as** <u>Where is Waldo</u>. **Cover up a large part of the page and start searching at the top with children's finger following the page sections from left to right, top to bottom.**
3. **Read the material aloud from a blackboard or flip chart in the same way, using a stick or laser pointer to follow the reading order.**
4. **Use a page of text, repeating each word as you would with the image.**

Cut up small pieces of Velcro and place one on the back of each cut up image and one on each image on the page. When the images match, use the Velcro to hold them in place as you search the page for more images.

Chapter 10
Language Skills

Children with special needs display a range of strengths and challenges when using and understanding language in the classroom. With instruction and guidance, children can learn to use language efficiently.

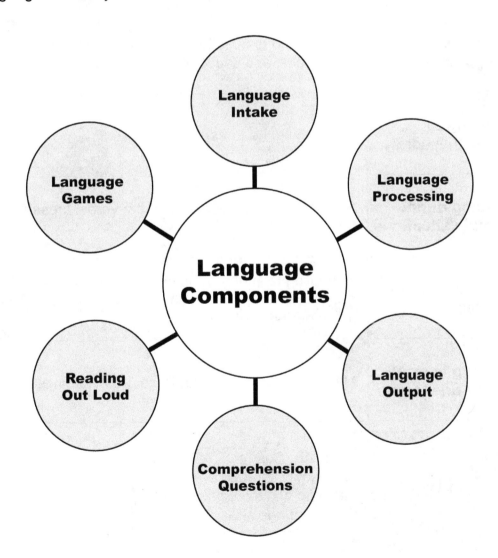

Language Skills Overview

When children are verbal, they may still display deficits in language comprehension and use. What appear to be obvious strengths in some children can mask underlying challenges.

STRENGTHS	CHALLENGES
Telling about events	Stating conclusions
Describing events, objects, people	Responding to questions that require inferences, deductions, and cause and effect
Responding to concrete questions	Maintaining the thread of a discussion
Conversing during predictable situations	Synthesizing the quickness of the verbal presentation with the visual intake
Taking turns during exchanges	Struggling to interpret the subtle intonations and the nuances in language, such as a louder tone emphasizing the importance of a topic
Conversing in small groups or one-to-one	Maintaining exchanges in large group settings

Focusing instruction on a theme has been shown to support understanding of a topic and helps to expand language skills.

Language Intake

Children with special needs may exhibit difficulties with the initial intake of information and require frequent exposure to verbal stimuli to process and register the information in their memory system.

STRATEGIES TO SUPPORT LANGUAGE INTAKE

» **Monitor the rate of speech when presenting information. Speaking too rapidly or too slowly can interfere with children's processing and registering of information.**

» **Use clear, concise statements to enable children to focus on the relevant details.**

» **Teach children to attend to changes in vocal intonations.**

   For example: *Point out to children and direct them to recognize that a louder tone or slower speech rate may indicate conveyance of important information.*

» **Give children a set of notes or a study guide during class lectures and direct children to give their full attention to the content of the lecture instead of worrying about taking notes.**

» **During discussions or lectures, encourage presenters to limit their movement around the classroom to help the student direct their attention to the speaker. This will help to limit distractions and changes in sound created by movement.**

» **When possible, have the student restate their understanding in their own words and provide clarification when necessary.**

Language Skills

Language Processing

Language Processing

Children with special needs may have difficulties maintaining and integrating the information in the working memory system for additional processing, storage, and application.

STRATEGIES TO SUPPORT LANGUAGE PROCESSING

» **Provide as much exposure to the verbal stimuli as possible and support with visual cues (study guides, visual reminders of a topic).**

» **Write key phrases and directions in a predetermined location on the white board or chalk board.**

» **Pre-teach vocabulary and information to give the student cues for the subject before a lecture or discussion. This will help to provide the additional exposure to the material.**

» **Teach children to use mapping techniques to take notes. This thinking tool helps children develop a mental framework, creates links among words and subjects, and lessens the demand on the cognitive resources needed to take notes.**

» **Have a student pair up with another student in order to receive support to help gather and understand the verbal presentation.**

Language Output

Because of the weaknesses with processing and registering of information, some children with special needs may exhibit difficulties organizing, accessing, and using language to express their ideas, their thought processes, their opinions, and their needs in a classroom setting.

STRATEGIES TO SUPPORT LANGUAGE OUTPUT

» **Use specific questions to help children frame their thoughts.**

» **Give children additional time to generate their thoughts. Research has indicated that teachers generally give approximately 3 seconds for children to respond. Children with special needs may need 10 or more seconds to gather their thoughts to respond.**

» **Give cues to prompt the student when they will be asked the question and the type of question they will be asked.**

For example:
Say, "John, after Sal answers this question, you will be asked next. Think about how ... is related to ...before answering." This will help cue the student to organize and prepare his thoughts before answering.

READING COMPREHENSION QUESTIONS

Connecting/Relating to Prior Knowledge
» Does this seem familiar to ….?
» Does this remind you of something you already know?
» How is this similar to ….?
» What do you already know about this topic?

Evidence
» How is it related to …?
» How do you support your idea?

Ordering and Sequencing
» What happened first, next, and then...?
» What were the steps?
» How long did it occur?
» How often did it occur?

Describing Own Thoughts
» How did you find the solution or answer?
» What were you thinking about as you worked through the problem or thought about the topic?

Elaborate
» What else can you say about...?
» How can you tell me more about …?

Clarification
» What do you mean by …?
» Help me to understand...?
» Can you explain?

Intent/Purpose/Overall Goal
» How come...?
» What were the reasons to …?
» What is the purpose of...?
» Why did you …?

Considering Other Ideas or Approaches
» How else...?
» Are there different ways to...?
» What other ways do you think could...?

Application
» Would this work? Why or why not?
» What other things do you think you could do?

Beliefs/Feelings/Opinions
» Why do you think this is important?
» Do you feel that this is important and why?
» Do you believe this will work? Why or why not?
» What is your opinion about... and why?
» Do you think ….matters? Why or why not?
» What are your feelings about this...?

Procedure/Follow Through
» What are you going to do next and why?
» Do you think … needs further investigation? Why or why not?
» What do you think needs to happen now?

Reading Out Loud

Read out loud on a daily basis. Reading out loud exposes children to the different rhythms of language and different uses of words and supports vocabulary and language comprehension. Also, reading out loud to children provides practice learning to sit and focus on a speaker.

- When selecting a book to read out loud to children, select one a little above their independent reading level. This will expose them to new vocabulary and pique their interest in a subject.

- Select a story connected to a topic that is studied in class. This will help to provide exposure to the topic through a different perspective.

- Vary the types of books you choose to read to the class. Read poetry, letters, biographies, informational texts, and a variety of fiction and narratives.

- When reading out loud, periodically stop and have children tell what they think will happen next or tell about their favorite character. This will encourage them to make connections to prior knowledge and to link ideas.

- When finishing a reading out loud session, make sure to stop at a high point. This will entice children to want to hear more of the story next time.

- Carefully monitor children's reactions during the read out loud sessions to help determine when to end a session and begin the next activity.

- Begin the next out loud reading session by reviewing what happened previously in the story. Use guiding questions to help the children gather and connect the information. This will help children engage with the story line.

- The amount of time to read to a class depends upon the age. Begin with 10 minutes of reading out loud to kindergartners and gradually increase the time. Children in the 2nd grade should be able to sit and listen to a story for about 15 minutes or longer; however this depends upon children's exposure and focus skills. It may be beneficial to read out loud for two short sessions during the day rather than one long one if children are young or still learning to sit and listen. Gradually increase the amount of time (up to 30 minutes) as children become able to sustain focus.

- Reading out loud is a useful activity to support transitions from high level activities to more focused academic activities, such as preparing children to shift focus on instruction after attending physical education class.

Language Skills

Reading Out Loud

INTRODUCING THE BOOK

» Tell the title, then ask: What do you think this book is about and why?

» What kind of book do you think this is (fiction, informational, biographical)?

» Do the title and cover illustration remind you of a story or book you have seen before?

WHILE READING THE BOOK

Fiction:

» Does the story sound like another story you have heard?

» Does the main character remind you of someone you know?

» Who do you think is the most interesting character and why?

» Where do you think this story is taking place? Does it remind you of a place you know?

Nonfiction:

» Do you think this topic is interesting/important?

» Why do you think the author chose to write about the person or event?

» What do you think were the important events?

» What do you think were the turning points that affected the events or the person's life?

REFLECTING ON THE STORY OR BOOK WHEN COMPLETED

Fiction:

» What do you think the author is trying to tell through this story?

» Why do you think the author chose to write this book?

» Would you read another story on this topic or by this author?

» What did the story mean to you?

» Do you have any questions or thoughts after hearing the story?

Nonfiction:

» Do you think the author portrayed the events accurately?

» What did you learn from hearing this book?

» Are you interested in reading more about this topic? Why or why not?

Language Games

During activity time, guide children to participate in games to support language skills. Games in the classroom need to be used as tools to learn the appropriate social skills as well as to support academic learning. These activities can be incorporated into language arts, writing, spelling, and reading instruction.

Working with games in the classroom can provide situations for children to practice using problem solving skills, language skills, and social skills, such as self-awareness, and learning to recognize nonverbal social cues. This simulates the skills children need to function in less structured environments.

Before working with games in the classroom, it is important to establish the classroom as a safe, nurturing environment that clearly defines the expectations of the interactions.

SUGGESTIONS FOR USING GAMES EFFECTIVELY IN THE CLASSROOM

» **Select developmentally appropriate games that clearly match the targeted skills. Games that are too complex or difficult to play will overwhelm children and can be hard to use as a teaching tool.**

» **Explicitly state the purpose of the game and the targeted skill. This will help to direct the focus on the learning and not the task.**

For example: State to the children, " You are going to practice with word categories; to do this we are going to play a word game..." Then clearly define the directions of the game and any changes to the instructions.

» **Competitiveness can interfere with the learning activity. It is necessary to direct the focus away from the winning of the game.**

» **Some children will need reassurance that it doesn't matter who wins or loses. It will be necessary to monitor children's reactions to the activity and to redirect if necessary.**

For example: If children become excited and begin to chant, " I am winning..." or use a put down such as calling the other players "loser", the situation will need immediate adult intervention. The correction will need to be implemented in accordance with the classroom rules.

Language Skills

Language Games

Language Games Ages 6 to 12

It is important to remember, when selecting a game, to think about children's skills as well as children's age. Sometimes, games have complex rules and multiple steps that can frustrate children and turn them away from the activity.

LISTENING SKILLS

» **To encourage careful listening and intake of information, play games like "Telephone" or "Granny's Suitcase" to practice listening and remembering the orally presented information.**

» **Sound games, making up riddles, rhymes, and tongue twisters provide language practice as well as practice discriminating the sounds in words, a foundational skill for efficient word reading.**

» **Have children repeat clapping or sound rhythms that increase in complexity.**

» **Play "Simon Says" using verbal directions.**

» **Play charades or have children pantomime to help link the nonverbal cues to language. This may also help them learn to become more attuned to the messages conveyed in gestures that co-occur with speech.**

» **Barrier games are also useful and can be used in pairs. This type of game requires one child to verbalize concisely an element of an object or picture and requires the partner to draw, build, or locate what the student is describing. The game <u>Creatures and Critters</u> is a barrier game designed for referential communication.**

VOCABULARY SKILLS

» Games like <u>Outburst, Jr.</u>, <u>Tri Bond</u>, <u>Kids</u>, <u>Blurt</u>, and <u>Apples to Apples</u> encourage children to make connections among words and to generate alternate words related to a topic.

» To visually link words to their meanings, select games like <u>Pictionary, Jr.</u> and <u>Guess-a-Doodle</u>.

REASONING AND LANGUAGE

» Games that encourage children to analyze information, select succinct language to ask questions to eliminate nonessential information to find an object or solution, or to analyze information, include <u>Guess Who</u>, <u>Secret Square</u>, and <u>Mystery Garden</u>.

who?   what?   when?   why?

» <u>Clue, Jr.</u> provides practice with deductive reasoning to find a solution. Other games that require deductive reasoning include <u>I Spy</u> and <u>20 Questions.</u>

NARRATIVE LANGUAGE

» To practice organizing thoughts to tell a story in a methodical manner, <u>The Storybook Game</u> and <u>Tell-a-Story</u> may be useful.

GENERAL KNOWLEDGE

» Games that require children to generate information and to understand questions include <u>Trivial Pursuit, Jr.</u>, <u>Cadoo</u>, <u>Cranium</u>, <u>Loaded Questions, Jr.</u>, and <u>Wit's End, Jr.</u>

Language Skills
Language Games

Language Games Ages 12 and Up

VOCABULARY AND FIGURATIVE LANGUAGE

» Other games for older children to practice with vocabulary, word relationships and meaning include <u>Loaded Questions</u>, <u>Wise and Otherwise</u>, <u>25 Words or Less</u>, and <u>Imatchaination</u>.

» Games like <u>Wordigo</u> and <u>Lexogon</u> work with vocabulary knowledge.

» Have children work with poetry, riddles, analogies, word chains, and mysteries made up for other children to solve to help practice using language in a variety of ways.

WORD STRUCTURE AND MEANING

» Have older children work with anagrams, create acronyms, and construct mysteries to have others solve.

» Games for older children to work with abstract language include <u>Picture This</u> and <u>Fiction Word Scrabble</u>. Read alternative play directions for <u>Fiction Word Scrabble</u>.

» Games that explore the changes in meaning and structure of words include <u>Anagramania</u>, <u>Word Thief</u>, <u>Beheaded</u>, <u>Scrabble</u>, <u>Derivation,</u> and <u>Keesdrow</u>.

○ *Example of an anagram*

CONTEXT AND NARRATIVES

» There are story telling and narrative games for older children to support their organization of language to concisely describe an event. Games include <u>Once Upon a Time</u> and <u>Nano Fictionary</u>.

Chapter 11
Mathematics

The effects of special needs could impact children's ability to encode verbal and visual information. Inefficient encoding could impede children's registration of information in memory and impact the integration of the information needed to form concepts. In addition, difficulties with the processing of visual-spatial information are associated with special needs. This could hinder children's ability to create mental representations to support problem solving needed in math.

Math Proficiency

According to the Mathematics Learning Study Committee of the National Research Council published in 2001 (Adding It Up, 2001, Washington, D.C.: National Academy Press, www. nap.edu or www.national-academies.org) children need to acquire five elements to become proficient in math.

THE FIVE COMPONENTS OF MATH PROFICIENCY

1. **Conceptual Understanding:**
   knowledge of the mathematical operations and their relationships

2. **Procedural Fluency:**
   ability to select, apply, and flexibly use the procedures to solve problems

3. **Strategic Competency:**
   ability to create, represent, and solve mathematical problems

4. **Adaptive Reasoning:**
   use of logical thought to demonstrate, explain, and verify the solutions

5. **Productive Disposition:**
   positive attitude toward mathematics that includes the understanding of the usefulness of math

Mathematics
Concept Knowledge

Concept Knowledge

Children need to grasp ideas that provide a foundation for subsequent learning and support a variety of tasks and procedures that go beyond a single activity. It is important for instruction to be focused around a central mathematical concept to enable children to develop understanding.

EXAMPLES OF CENTRAL MATH CONCEPTS

» **Number**
» **Sequence and Pattern**
» **Sets and Set Relationships**
» **Operations**
» **Representation of Quantity in Numeric and Nonnumeric Forms**

» *Shape, Space, and Geometric Forms*
» *Money*
» *Time, Movement, and Speed*
» *Measurement – Standard and Nonstandard Units*
» *Data Representation and Interpretation*

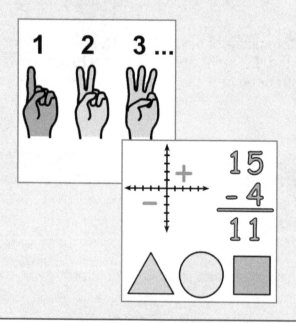

Some children need to have adult mediated experiences to help them develop the necessary mathematical concepts to support their learning. Pointing out specific information, the relationships, and encouraging children to tell about their thought processes helps to stimulate learning in math.

Exploring Concepts

Children benefit from using a variety of objects and materials to explore mathematical ideas independently. For example, have small blocks or other objects accessible in the classroom for children to explore during activity or free time.

▶▶▶**Activities:**

- Have children complete puzzles, build using a variety of materials such as wooden blocks and empty household cartons, or make inventions. Young children can incorporate their inventions into imaginary play.

- Provide children with a problem to solve and use open-ended questions to guide their exploration of the targeted concept.

    Example: *"How many different patterns can you locate on the number chart?" "How can you use the number chart to solve …?" "Do you find patterns helpful to solve problems? Why or why not?" Asking questions stimulates thinking.*

Hundreds Chart

1	2	3	4	5	6	7	8	9	10
11	12	13	14	15	16	17	18	19	20
21	22	23	24	25	26	27	28	29	30
31	32	33	34	35	36	37	38	39	40
41	42	43	44	45	46	47	48	49	50
51	52	53	54	55	56	57	58	59	60
61	62	63	64	65	66	67	68	69	70
71	72	73	74	75	76	77	78	79	80
81	82	83	84	85	86	87	88	89	90
91	92	93	94	95	96	97	98	99	100

Hundreds Chart

* See Appendix "Hundreds Chart"

Mathematics
Concept Knowledge

- Give children opportunities to explain their thoughts. If they are unable to link the language to the concept, provide children with the label. For example, if a child is trying to explain the concept of addition but cannot verbalize the word "higher" or "more", use a vertical number line and specifically point to the numbers as they increase. State that the numbers are getting more/higher. This reinforces the concept visually and links it to the language.

- Reinforce the necessity of mathematics. For example, explain that children need to learn to estimate in order to judge time and estimate space when they are learning to maintain personal boundaries during social exchanges

- Incorporate math into other academic domains. For example, if studying cities in social studies, have a visual that demonstrates the different measurement units and link the concept of measurement to the different types of building and structures found in cities.

- Provide frequent review and explicitly connect new concepts to prior knowledge. Use verbal cues such as, "Last week we studied..., this week we will expand on the idea..." to help children link to prior knowledge.

- Incorporate books during read out loud or during language arts that target math concepts or ideas. This will encourage children to think about math across academic domains and provide opportunities for discussion.

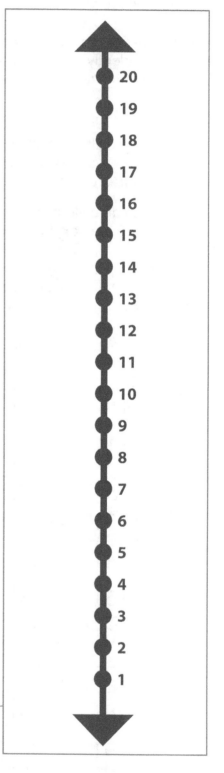

Vertical Number Line

Procedural Knowledge

Concepts and procedures are connected and often learned simultaneously. Concept understanding provides children with the reasons why numbers, shapes, and values can be transformed. Procedural knowledge tells how to manipulate the concepts to alter the amounts, values, and forms to solve the problems.

▶▶▶**Teaching Strategies:**

- Direct children on how to analyze the math questions and select the pertinent information.

- Instruct children on how to represent information in different ways. For example, have children generate different ways to show 7, such as 3+4 or 8-1. Show them how to select the most efficient method to represent an amount in relation to the problem they are trying to solve. Math Mahjong* is a computer game designed to practice this skill. Teach children to recognize the specific language that indicates an operation or procedure.

- Guide children to recognize the similarities between an equation and a spoken sentence. Direct them to translate the spoken sentence into the symbolic form. It is important that children understand the meaning of equals. The equal sign does not mean an answer, it means that the sides of the equation separated by the equal sign need to have the same value. This will help to lay the foundation for algebraic thinking as children move toward more complex math.

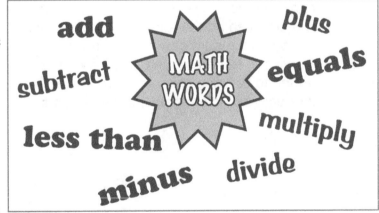

- Teach children the relationships among addition, subtraction, multiplication, and division. For example, show children how to use fact family relationships such as subtraction to locate a missing number in an addition problem.**

Mathematics

Procedural Knowledge

▶▶▶**Computation Activities:**

- Play games to support computation fluency. Card games such as "War", "Addition War", and "21" provide practice with these facts.

- Domino games can be used to practice addition and subtraction, as well as used for sorting, forming number sets, and patterning.

- The Quizmo game series has versions to practice math skills in areas such as number recognition, money, telling time, and fractions, as well as basic addition, subtraction, multiplication, and division.

- Trilemma and Equate provide practice with math computation and forming number sentences.

- Use computer games to practice math facts and skills. Suggestions for computer games that focus on math include Mia's Math Adventure, Learn to Play Chess with Fritz and Chester, Genius, Crazy Machines and Wacky Contraptions, and Math Mahjong.

- Teach older children strategies to assist with fact recall. For example, children can remember easily a number added to 10. Children can add to ten, but remember to +1 to find the sum of a number added to 11 or -1 to remember the sum of a number added to 9. Once children learn to use this strategy, they can apply it to other sums.

Math Mahjong ○——

WHEN INTRODUCING MATH STRATEGIES

» *Link the strategy to the targeted concept.*

» *Teach children how and when to use the strategy.*

» *Provide guided practice for children to use the strategy.*

» *Once children are proficient in using the strategy, introduce a new one and guide children how to select the appropriate strategy from their choices.*

▶▶▶**Number Activities:**

- Have children sort coins according to their amounts. This will help them recognize coins and provide exposure to their value.

- Play money exchange games to help children work with place value, equivalent amounts, and carrying and borrowing.

- To practice with number recognition and basic counting skills for young children, play games like <u>Chutes and Ladders</u>, <u>Hi Ho Cherry-O</u>, <u>Memory</u>, <u>Go Fish</u>, and <u>Crazy-8s</u>.

- Drilling with flash cards can help with math fact knowledge. To support children's generation of the equation, present a card with a signal digit written on it such as 9. Then ask children to compute a problem, such as "multiply by 3". Have children state the answer. This will help children generate the equation they are solving.

Mathematics

Procedural Knowledge

▶▶▶**Spatial Skills Activities:**

- Have children complete origami, make paper airplanes, and participate in paper folding activities, like wrapping presents, to recognize common fractions terms, size estimation, and spatial skills. Have children participate in tasks that use math, such as cooking or woodworking.

- Play checkers or chess with children to explore patterns and spatial skills. The games Master Mind and Battleship also provide practice with patterning, logic, and spatial skills.

- Encourage children to build with a variety of materials, such as Legos, or build domino rallies to practice with spatial relationships.

- Have children explore tessellations or complete tangram or pentomino puzzles to explore visual patterns. Have children make tessellation stencils to replicate the patterns or color the patterns in different ways.

- Teach children finger-string games such as Cat's Cradle. This helps with spatial skills, following directions, and sequencing the steps to complete the form.

▶▶▶**Student Aids:**

- To minimize visual distractions and confusion, limit the number of problems presented on a page or worksheet. Try to keep 4-5 problems on a worksheet.

- Keep worksheets free of unnecessary decorations or information. This will help to maintain focus on the direction of the task.

- Teach children how to make cue cards to help remember the steps to complete computation.

- To support fact knowledge in the classroom, provide access to number charts, multiplication grids, and calculators.

- Use grid paper* to help children line up problems and limit visual confusion.

Division Steps

Divide

Multiply

Subtract

Move Right

Bring Down

Check for Repeat

$$2 + 6 = 8$$

$$5 + 4 = 9$$

$$1 + 6 = 7$$

Using Manipulatives

Use manipulatives during Instruction to demonstrate the targeted concept.

▶▶▶ **When using manipulatives it is beneficial to consider:**

- Match the materials to the concept being modeled.

  Example: *If using manipulatives to introduce addition, select individual counters instead of bundled sticks or rods. The stick bundles can be interpreted as one group or an amount determined by the number in that bundle.*

- If introducing a new material, allow children time to explore with the objects before using them for teaching purposes. This will provide opportunities for children to explore concepts as well as remove the novelty of the materials.

- Clearly state the purpose of the manipulatives. This helps to link the concept to its purpose as well as lead toward learning about a procedure.

- Once children efficiently demonstrate the concept using the manipulatives, gradually model how to represent the concept in different way, such as using pictures or symbols.

- Gradually phase out the use of manipulatives as children master the concept.

- As children become proficient with the concept, provide novel problems to solve that use that concept.

LIST OF USEFUL MANIPULATIVES FOR MATHEMATICS INSTRUCTION

- » *Base 10 blocks*
- » *Unifix cubes*
- » *Tangrams*
- » *Pattern blocks*
- » *Attribute blocks*
- » *Dual colored counters*
- » *Set of unit blocks*
- » *Variety of dice (include regular six sided dice, four sided dice, and octahedrons)*
- » *Playing cards*
- » *Dominoes (include 9 dots and/or 12 dots)*
- » *Geometric patterns or shape templates*
- » *Buttons or other objects*
- » *Sorting trays or mats*
- » *Containers in different sizes*
- » *Colored paper in a variety of sizes and shades*

These items can be used in math classes across grade levels. Most of these manipulatives can be purchased at a local school supply store or online. Examples of materials that can be made or collected include sorting mats, pattern templates, containers, scraps of different colored papers left over from wrapping paper, envelopes, or greeting cards, and dice collected from old games that are no longer used.

Chapter 12
Study Skills

Teachers, caregivers, and other professionals working with children need to work together to provide support. This requires frequent contact between home and school. This lets children know that the adults are interested and supportive of their progress in school. Teachers and caregivers also need to establish an effective communication system. Other professionals, such as social workers, counselors, and therapists, need to be informed of the children's progress in school. This can be done through meetings or written updates.

▶▶▶ Teachers and Caregivers Need To:

- Agree at the beginning of the school year the type of information that would be beneficial to be sent home in order to support children – e.g. information about behavior, specific academic information, social interactions, or medical updates.

- Agree on the frequency of the communications home – such as daily, weekly, biweekly, or as needed.

- Agree upon the method of communications – e.g. email, notes home, telephone conversations, weekly meetings.

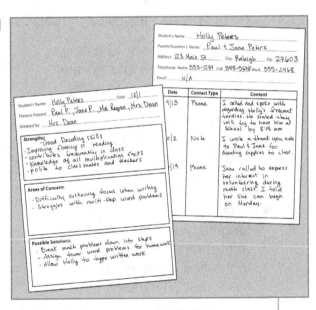

Conference & Communication Logs

Teachers and therapists need to exchange information as soon as possible if there are changes in the children's plan, program, or other information that would impact their progress.

Study Skills
General Suggestions

General Suggestions

Teachers can help children with managing and completing homework assignments.

▶▶▶ **Suggestions to help children with homework:**

- Maintain a consistent homework schedule.

- Give parents a syllabus or a homework schedule that they can keep at home. Some classes have a web site that post the weekly homework.

- Review the assignment with children. Ask children to tell about the assignment and provide any clarification they may need.

- Help children to remember to bring their books home. Put a check list in their book bag or tape a reminder in their locker or storage space at school.

- Provide extra copies of instructional support charts at home, such as vertical number lines, multiplication tables, number boards, and math grids*.

- Assign homework as a way to provide practice and review of previously learned skills. Establish the purpose of the assignment. State the expectation for completion of the assignment. This will help to engage children in the assignment.

- Keep homework assignment lengths developmentally appropriate. For example, children in the first grade need to have no more that 20 minutes of work an evening. Children who have long, tedious homework assignments become frustrated and disengaged with the learning process.

Class	Homework	Finished
Writing	Chapter 3 Answer Questions 1-3	✓
Reading	Rewrite rough draft of book report	✓
MATH	1) Fraction Worksheet 2) 10 Minutes of Flashcards	✓
Science	Study Chapter 12	
History	Define "Industrial Revolution" and give 5 examples	
Key-boarding	Type worksheet	

*Homework Chart***

* See Appendix "Vertical Number Line", "Multiplication Table", "Grid Paper"
** See Appendix "Homework Chart"

Supports at Home

To help with homework issues at home, teachers and caregivers need to discuss the patterns of homework assignments and the expectations regarding homework.

▶▶▶ **Some general reasons children are reluctant to do homework include:**

- Fatigue at the end of a long school day

- Frustration caused by not understanding the assignment

- Forgetting the materials needed to complete the assignment

- Assignments that are too difficult

- Competing interests such as video games

- Over-scheduled with after school activities

- Emotional and behavioral issues

Encourage caregivers to discuss any difficulties they may have with children completing work at home. If homework becomes a struggle, discuss with the caregiver the issues that could impact homework. There are many reasons that could cause the difficulties. Help to analyze why homework may be a chore and make suggestions accordingly.

Suggestions for Caregivers

Teachers can provide suggestions to the caregivers to help children with homework.

SUGGESTIONS FOR CAREGIVERS

» **Keep a class list that children can call if they forget their homework. Have children exchange contact information with a peer so they can call if they need help or information about homework assignments or classroom events.**

» **Keep materials, such as paper, sharpened pencils, calculators, rulers, and other tools, in an accessible location. This will help with organization.**

» **Establish a homework time to help the student develop efficient study habits.**

» **Set boundaries with children about the amount of help they receive. Sometimes children will rely on adult assistance to complete tasks that they can do independently. Allocate a certain number of problems that children must do before checking in with an adult.**

» **If children need breaks, use sand timers or analogue clocks to help monitor the work time.**

» **Have the student take a quick active break before starting again, such as shooting 10 baskets or riding his/her bike around the block twice.**

» **Before going to bed, have children pack their book bag and set it in an obvious location so they will not forget it the next day.**

Test Taking Strategies

Because of the high stakes of testing, many children with and without special needs become anxious about taking tests. Preparing children to know what to expect on the test, how to maneuver the test format, and how to analyze the questions may help them to become less anxious and improve performance.

▶▶▶ Test Taking Practice

- Some children become overwhelmed with filling in the bubbles on the answer sheets. Provide opportunities for children to become acquainted with completing the answer sheets.

- Teach children how to maneuver the test layout. Show them how to recognize the direction symbols, bolded information, charts, and highlighted material.

- If the visual layout of the test booklet is too cluttered, encourage children to fold the booklet so there is only one page showing at one time. If scratch paper is allowed, have them cover up the questions they are not working on to minimize visual distraction.

- Expose children to the different time allotments. Use regular class time or independent work to help acclimate to the time length.

  Example: If they have thirty minutes to work on a section, monitor the time as if it is a testing session.

- Teach children to recognize the key words, terms, and common phrases that are used in tests.

- Often children overlook the stop and start marks, so point them out to the students.

- Teach children to skip ahead to other questions if they don't know the answer. Do the hardest questions last.

Sample Bubble Test

- Practice how to analyze the test questions. Instruct children about the different types of questions

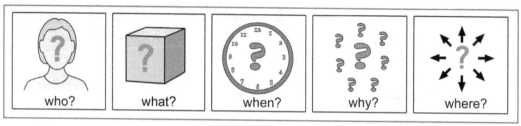

> » *What – may ask for a concrete response or a specific detail.*
>
> » *Why/How – may be seeking a reason or an inference.*
>
> » *When – may ask for a response that refers to historical time, a specific date or hour, or a general reference.*
>
> » *Where – may ask for a location or a setting.*
>
> » *Who – may require a specific name, a character, or a subject.*

- Show children how to make educated guesses.

  For example:

  > » *Teach children how to eliminate unnecessary responses in multiple choice selections.*
  >
  > » *Have them recognize the wording most commonly used in testing to support their guessing between two closely related answers (e.g. 'all of the time' versus 'some of the time').*
  >
  > » *Show children how to use previous answers or information to guide responses to subsequent questions.*

- When practicing for the test, directly point out how the test is similar to things they learned in class. This will help children to recognize familiar elements and to connect to prior knowledge.

- Guide children to use their problem solving strategies when working with practice problems, such as what type of diagram or pictorial representation will support solving a math problem.

- Provide caregivers information about the tests, the state's rules on testing, scoring, and how to gather samples of the testing format. Keeping caregivers informed about the rules and regulations may help to lessen the stress families feel if they are uncomfortable with the use and purposes of the standardized testing scores.

KEY WORDS FOR READING

Main Idea

» This passage is mostly about...

» The central idea is....

View Points

» The author wrote this passage to...

» The purpose of the passage is...

Specific Details

» According to the passage...

» Give an example of ...

KEY WORDS FOR MATHEMATICS

Number Sense

» Give the number nearest to...

» Round to...

» The number greater than, less than, and/or equal to...

» This digit shows the value (For example, in 345, the 3 holds the place for hundreds, the 4 holds a place for tens, the 5 for ones).

Computation

» This number sentence is the same as ...

» Which symbol means to _____ ? (Ex, +/- or 1)

» In all   (sums)

» Find the difference

Study Skills

Test Taking

Test Taking Accommodations

Standardized Testing

The purpose of standardized testing is to compare children's functioning or academic performance to the results on the same tasks completed by subjects who are considered to represent the population. The scores can be compared in order to make deductions regarding the children's performance. School systems use a variety of standardized tests, such as the Standford Tests and the Iowa Basic Skills Tests, to measure their student's performance in academics.

Testing Accommodations

Some children will require testing accommodations to take the standardized tests. Some accommodations will not affect the scores and enable the administrators to make comparisons about the children's performance based on an age group or a grade level. However, some adjustments to the testing setting, administration of the test, and/or the test presentation may influence results, thus invalidating the score comparisons.

EXAMPLES OF GENERAL ACCOMMODATIONS THAT MAY NOT INFLUENCE THE STANDARDIZATION OF THE TEST SCORES

Test Setting
- » Small group
- » Special education classroom
- » Specific lighting conditions
- » Preferential setting
- » Slant board to assist with writing
- » Study carrel
- » Individualized administration
- » Frequent monitored breaks
- » Extended time

Presentation of Test
- » Large print materials
- » Braille
- » Cover overlays or templates
- » Low vision aids
- » Sign the directions
- » Adaptive Listening devices
- » Explain or paraphrase the directions for clarity
- » Repetition of directions
- » Materials presented with contrast or tactile cues

Student Responses
- » Technological apparatus (e.g. Braille writer)
- » Mark answers in test booklet
- » Test recorder
- » Point to answer
- » Verbal responses
- » Adaptive writing tools (e.g. pencil grip)

* It is important to check with your state department of education or test publisher to determine if the accommodations alter the standardization of the test results.

Appendix

Contents:

Picture Cards
Classroom Picture Cards
Behavior Picture Cards

Teacher Forms
Classroom Observation Form
Teacher Observation Form
Behavior Management Form

Classroom Tools
How to Draw a Dog
How to Draw a House
Conference Log
Communication Log
"Dear Parents" Letter
Self-Monitoring Sheet
Desk Chart
Homework Chart
Visual Clock
Flower Chart
Social Play Action Figure
Classroom Rights Printout

Problem Solving
Semantic Feature Analysis
Brainstorming Maps
Organizing Maps
Processing Maps

Literacy Tools
Reading Organizer
Reading Form
Reading Response Form
Nonfiction Report
Journal Writing
Story Organizer

Writing Tools
Stop-N-Go Writing Paper
Lined Writing Paper

Math Helpers
Hundreds Chart
Multiplication Table
Vertical Number Chart
Graph Paper

Classroom Picture Cards

	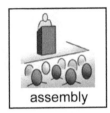			
art	assembly	backpack	beanbag chair	bleachers

books on tape	bus	bus driver	cafeteria	call on

chalkboard	change class	check schedule	circle time	class

classroom	communication folder	cubbyhole	desk	ear phones

field trip	fire drill	gymnasium	hallway	hang up jacket
				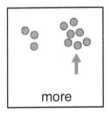
homework	library	line up	lunch	more
	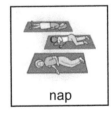			
music	nap	raise hand	recess	time-out

 ask
 calm down
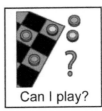 Can I play?
 cheat
 choose

 clap
 congratulations
 cry
 danger
 discuss

 don't chase
 don't tease
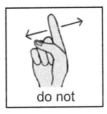 do not
 follow directions
 give

 goodbye
 good game
 hello
 help
 high five

 hit
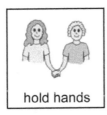 hold hands
 How are you?
 hug
 I'm fine

 I'm sorry
 I don't know
 I don't like that
 I don't understand
 I like that

 I want
 laugh
 leave me alone
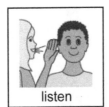 listen
 need a break

Classroom Observation Form

Sample completed form (Front):

Classroom Observation: Date of Observation: 2/3/07   Observer: Mrs. C

Student: _C.J._   Chronological Age: 6 yrs

Grade Level: _1st_   Class: _Math_   Teacher/Instructor: Mrs. T

Beginning Time: 9:40am   Ending Time: 10:00am

What are the questions or concerns about the student's behavior? _Does C.J. have difficulties in a large group setting tha effects his learning in math?_

Classroom Layout

What activity or class is being observed? _whole class instruction on addition, review_

What is the pace of the lesson? _Rapid. Students appear to maintain pace._

What is the student's affect during the lesson? _CJ continues to attract his neighors attention & seems unaware of instruction_

What is the teacher/s attitude toward the student? _Friendly._

How does the student interact in the classroom? _Student moves easily to retrieve books and materials._

Classroom Observation Form

Sample completed form (Back):

Is the student engaged with the lesson or activity – asking questions, attentive, and/or focused?

Student seems disengaged

Does the student understand the objectives of the task/lesson? _CJ. responds when asked orally to complete problem._

Does the student understand the directions? _yes._

Has the student approached the task/lesson systematically? _Not observed._

What type of assistance does the student require? _Frequent reminders / redirection_

Did the student use self-compensatory strategies? _Not observed._

Are there accommodations to help the student in class? _Not observed._

Concerns	Recommendations
-missing out during instruction because he is socializing w/ students near him.	- Relocate seat to an outer corner to minimize distractions
-no concerns about addition skills - Math skills need to be monitored.	-monitor math progress closely after seat relocation.

Conclusion: _C.J. is seated in the middle row, close to friends. During class time, C.J. is interacting w/ the friends and is distracted. CJs desk will be moved to the front to limit social distractions. Additional evaluation of math skills may be warranted._

Classroom Observation Form

Classroom Observation: **Date of Observation:** / /   **Observer:** _____

Student: _____   **Chronological Age:** _____

Grade Level: _____   **Class:** _____   **Teacher/Instructor:** _____

Beginning Time: _____   **Ending Time:** _____

What are the questions or concerns about the student's behavior? _____

_____

_____

Classroom Layout

_____

What activity or class is being observed?_____

What is the pace of the lesson? _____

What is the student's affect during the lesson? _____

What is the teacher/s attitude toward the student? _____

How does the student interact in the classroom? _____

Classroom Observation Form

Date of Observation: _____

Is the student engaged with the lesson or activity – asking questions, attentive, and/or focused?
_____

Does the student understand the objectives of the task/lesson? _____

Does the student understand the directions? _____

Has the student approached the task/lesson systematically? _____

What type of assistance does the student require? _____

Did the student use self-compensatory strategies? _____

Are there accommodations to help the student in class? _____

Concerns	Recommendations

Conclusion: _____

_____

_____

_____

Teacher Observation Form

Sample completed form:

Student's Name: CW	Date of Observation: January 2007

Date of Birth: January 2000   Observer: Mr. Jones

Chronological Age: 7 years   Grade Level: 1st

Questions regarding Behavioral Concerns:
- Are there times of the day when CW becomes more disruptive in class?
- Does CW have difficulties with task changes?
- How does CW interact during structured class time compared to unstructured class time?

Description of Behavior	Time of Observation	Setting/ Class	Frequency	Trigger/ Antecedent	Comments
Hits other students.	8:00-8:30 am	Entering the Classroom	5 occurrences	Lots of movement in the hall. Transitioning from the bus to the room.	CW appears confused when entering the classroom. It seems hard for CW to orientate in the classroom Seems to think others are hitting him.
Calls other students names and/or hits other students.	10:00-10:30 am	Cooperative Learning Groups	7 occurrences	When CW's ideas are not always accepted.	CW seems to become frustrated when his ideas are not used.
Hits other students and calls students names	12:00-12:30 pm	Playground/ Recess	7 occurrences	When CW is not picked first to play on a team. When CW's ideas are not used.	CW becomes angry when his suggestions are not used. Thinks other kids are ignoring him.
Hits other students.	2:15-2:30 pm	Getting ready to go home	3 occurrences	Student's gathering in a small area. Transitioning to go home.	CW seems to become disoriented when in a group with a lot of movement

Summary of Findings:

CW seems to react more toward the amount of structure provided during a class segment rather than a specific time of day. Class time that requires students to work some independently or unstructured time are challenges for CW. CW struggles in settings that require filtration of his surroundings. He seems to become overwhelmed when placed in groups and required to synthesize the verbal and visual intake in order to interact in these situations. It is difficult for CW to manage in groups where there are a variety of activities occurring. When CW becomes angry in these situations, he lashes out at the other students. CW has a tendency to misinterpret accidental contacts with another student. He perceives a bump from another student as being intentional. He will react to this by hitting the student who he thinks intentionally bumped him. CW seems to perceive constant rejection from peers when his ideas are not accepted. Negotiating peer interactions seem to be difficult for him.

Suggestions:

From the information gathered, a behavior management plan will need to be created. Strategies as well as the need for the appropriate type of adult support and facilitation will need to be discussed in order to devise the appropriate plan to help CW learn to maneuver the classroom.

Also, an evaluation by the school counselor or psychologist may be needed to investigate CW's social perception and difficulties.

Teacher Observation Form

Student's Name: _____   Date of Observation: _____

Date of Birth: _____   Observer: _____

Chronological Age: _____   Grade Level: _____

Teacher: _____

Questions regarding Behavioral Concerns:

_____

_____

_____

Description of Behavior	Time of Observation	Setting/ Class	Frequency	Trigger/ Antecedent	Comments

Summary of Findings:

_____

_____

_____

Behavior Management Form

A behavior management plan can have any format. For illustration, an example design is shown here.

1. Create a list of goals that target problem behaviors.
2. Define the target replacement behaviors for these goals.
3. Use student feedback to encourage replacement behaviors.
4. Define the teacher monitoring methods.
5. Communicate with the family to coordinate efforts.
6. Follow through and phase out the monitoring.

Sample of a Completed Behavior Management Plan

Date: January 2007   **Duration of Intervention:** Approx. 3 months

Student: CW   **Class/Grade:** 1st grade

Goals:

1. CW will not become disruptive during task transitions
2. CW will not exhibit aggressive behaviors toward other students when he becomes anxious
3. CW will regulate his reactions to the classroom environment

CW's reactions are triggered when there are changes in the schedule, changes in classroom routines, and during unstructured play time.

Target Replacement Behaviors:

1. Signal to teacher when overwhelmed.
2. Use words when angry.
3. Keep hands to yourself. Keep hands away from other children when angry.
4. Learn to go to a quiet area independently when needing to calm down.
5. Go to an adult to ask for help when transitions or peer negotiations are difficult.

Student Feedback:

1. CW responds well to acknowledgement. Use statements to connect the positive actions and provide verbal recognition when he is meeting his goals.
2. A desk chart will be created with stickers to reward replacement behavior. If CW receives three stickers at the end of the day, he will be able to select a favorite activity from the reward survey to complete during activity time.
3. If CW does not meet the criteria of three stickers at the end of the day, the teacher will present him with choices of activities to select during unstructured time, or he may need to use that time to make up the work he missed.
4. Story boards and discussions will be utilized with CW to discuss the behavior incident as soon as he is able to discuss the problem. With the aid of the instructor, the problem will be reviewed and supportive options for next time created.
5. If CW cannot transition without assistance, a teacher will facilitate class changes. This may involve using tools such as handing CW a visual card to demonstrate transition time.
6. Time out intervention will be taught. If CW refuses to interact appropriately he will be directed away from the current activity. He will need to make up at another time any academic instruction he missed. This may have to occur during an unstructured time. However, it should not entail the entire free time period.
7. Natural consequences, such as using a waiting chair, will be used as much as possible. Care should be taken not to embarrass the child by singling him out for punishment

Methods to Monitor:

1. Behavior will be monitored on a daily basis.
2. Tally charts using the desk chart form will be recorded by the child and collected each day and discussed.
3. Behavioral interventions will be monitored through teacher checklists and observations and anecdotal notes.
4. Information will be summarized on a weekly basis.

Family Communication:

1. Daily notes will be sent in CW's communication or school folder.
2. A weekly summary of the behavior will be emailed to the family.
3. Information sent to CW's family will include how often he signaled the instructor, the effectiveness of the redirection, and the use of the tally and sticker system.
4. A weekly summary will consist of the current week's progress and will compare to prior weeks. It will note any intervention changes.

Follow Through:

1. The family has indicated they are working with a therapist on self-regulation and behavior management at home. Therapy is focusing on helping CW recognize feelings and select appropriate responses. The therapist will consult and work with CW's instructors to help maintain a consistent management plan and interventions.
2. Bi-weekly emails with CW's therapist will occur to review CW's progress and make necessary adjustments to his behavior plan.
3. A meeting with parents, teachers, and therapists will be convened in four weeks to review progress and adjust the behavior plan if necessary.
4. When CW reaches his goals, a method for phase out will be determined based on the time he took to learn the behaviors and his dependency on each particular feedback technique.

Behavior Management Plan

Date: _____   Duration of Intervention: _____

Student: _____   Class/Grade: _____

Goals:

1. _____

2. _____

3. _____

Target Replacement Behaviors:

1. _____

2. _____

3. _____

Student Feedback:

1. _____

2. _____

3. _____

Behavior Management Plan

Methods to Monitor:

1. _____

2. _____

3. _____

Family Communication:

1. _____

2. _____

3. _____

Follow Through:

1. _____

2. _____

3. _____

How to Draw a Dog

How to Draw a House

Communication Home

Conference Logs, Communication Logs, and Dear Parent letters are a great way to keep track of the communication between parents and teachers.

Student's Name: Holly Peters   Date: 12/1

Persons Present: Paul P., Jane P., Mr. Regan, Mrs. Dean

Initiated by: Mrs. Dean

Strengths:
- Good Decoding skills
- Improving fluency in reading
- contributes frequently in class
- Knowledge of all multiplication facts
- polite to classmates and teachers

Areas of Concern:
- Difficulty sustaining focus when writing
- Struggles with multi-step word problems

Possible Solutions:
- Break math problems down into steps
- Assign fewer word problems for homework
- Allow Holly to type written work

Sincerely, Mrs. Dean

Student's Name: Holly Peters

Parent/Guardian's Name: Paul & Jane Peters

Address: 123 Main St.   City: Raleigh   Zip: 27603

Telephone: Home 555-1234 Cell 555-5678 Work 555-2468

Email: N/A

Date	Contact Type	Content
9/13	Phone	I called and spoke with regarding Holly's frequent tardies. He stated they will try to have him at school by 8:15 am
10/2	Note	I wrote a thank you note to Paul & Jane for donating supplies to class.
10/19	Phone	Jane called to express her interest in volunteering during math class. I told her she can begin on Monday.

Rules
- Follow directions the first time given
- Complete assignments
- Remain in your assigned seat
- Request permission to speak
- Keep hands and feet to yourself

Rewards
Daily- praise, smiles, high-fives, and more
Weekly- computer time, free time, certificates, and more
Monthly- themed luncheons (e.g. "Picnic in the Park," Day at the Beach")
Quarterly- field trips, grade level celebration

Consequences
- Green Light = Good to go!
- Yellow Light = Warning
- Red Light = Note home
- Lights Out (or No Lights) = Note home + isolated lunch

* All students will begin each day on green.

Conference Log

Student's Name: _____ Date: _____

Persons Present: _____

Initiated by: _____

Strengths:

Areas of Concern:

Possible Solutions:

Communication Log

Student's Name: _____

Parent/Guardian's Name: _____

Address: _____ City: _____ Zip: _____

Telephone: Home _____ Cell _____ Work _____

Email: _____

Date	Contact Type	Content

Dear Parents...

We are off to a fantastic start! The students seem enthusiastic and eager to tackle the new school year and the challenges that may arise. As your child's teacher, I will do my part in creating a safe and fun learning environment.

To ensure a successful school year, please familiarize yourself with our classroom rules, as well as the rewards and consequences associated with them. If you have any questions, feel free to call me or stop by the classroom.

Sincerely, _____

Rules

Rewards

Consequences

Self-Monitoring Sheet for Older Students

- Explain to the student the reasons she is learning to monitor her own behavior. Discuss how this will help her become more independent.

- Discuss with the student the goals and target replacement behaviors.

- Review the rating scale you will use with the student.

- Each instructor will need to remind the student to complete the self-monitoring sheet until it becomes a habit.

- At the end of the day, discuss with the student how she did. What areas were difficult and why?

- Gather the data sheets and chart the information. Each week review the student performance and guide the student to reflect upon what was challenging.

- For this method, the teacher does not rate the student for each class. This is to be an instructional approach to help the older student become more reflective and to help teach the student to monitor her own behavior.

- However, it can be useful for the instructor to rate the student in each area and compare their observations with the student's observations. This can provide additional feedback and help the student to understand perspectives.

- The student will need to be corrected when necessary as well as receive acknowledgement or consequences when necessary.

Name: _Sandra_   Date: _December 10_

Using a scale from 3 to 1, rate how you did in each class.
3 = great
2 = ok
1 = oops

Target	MATH	Language Arts	GYM	Science
Waited for teacher to finish talking before responding	3	2	3	3
Counted to 10 and thought about my answer before responding	1	1	2	2
Used appropriate tone of voice	3	2	2	3

How would you describe your performance today?

OKay.

Was it harder to meet the targets in some classes more than others? Why or why not?

Languge arts class was hard because there are too many students.

What do you think would help you next time?

If Mrs. Carl would talk slower, I would listen much better.

Self-Monitoring Sheet

Name:_____ **Date:** _____

Using a scale from 3 to 1, rate how you did in each class.
3 = great
2 = ok
1 = oops

Target				

How would you describe your performance today?

_____

_____

_____

Was it harder to meet the targets in some classes more than others? Why or why not?

_____

_____

_____

What do you think would help you next time?

_____

_____

_____

Desk Chart

A desk chart is a way to monitor student progress on a behavior goal. It can be used as a method of feedback to allow a child to gauge his success in modifying problem behavior. Using tally marks, a student will receive a mark when he is following target behaviors. He will need to have three tally marks after each activity to receive a sticker for that class period.

Name: Kathy G. **Date:** October 12

Action	1	2	3	Sticker
Tell teacher when over whelmed	✓			
Use words when angry	✓	✓	✓	😄
Keep hands to your self				
Go to a quiet area to calm down	✓			
Ask for help when changes bother you	✓	✓		

Desk Chart

Name: _____   **Date:** _____

Action	1	2	3	Sticker

Homework Chart

- Establish a routine to turn in homework. Have students place assignments in the "in" basket as they enter the classroom.

- Use a weekly syllabus when assigning homework. Send a copy to the families each week, and post one in the classroom.

- Maintain a homework routine. Keep homework routines simple and manageable.

- Establish an organizational system with the student. Provide assistance until the student can manage the system.

- Gradually phase out the support as the student becomes more independently organized.

Week of __APRIL 10__

	Monday	Tuesday	Wednesday	Thursday	Friday	Weekend
MATH	pages 27-42	pages 42-52	Pages 53-60	Problems 1-4 page 63	Pages 64-70	Finish Chapter 14
Language Arts	Spelling- make study cards	Spelling- write sentences	Spelling- complete crossword	Study for test		Spelling Game
Reading	Read for 20 minutes	Read for 20 minutes	Read for 20 minutes	Read for 20 minutes	Read for 20 minutes	

Homework Chart

Week of _____

	Monday	Tuesday	Wednesday	Thursday	Friday	Weekend

Visual Clock

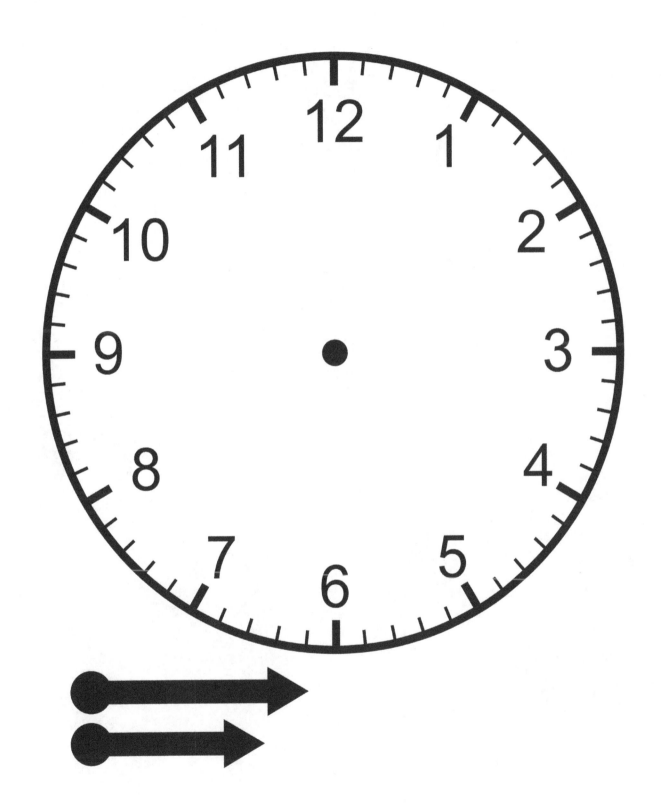

Flower Chart

- Use the flower chart during an activity to monitor the interactions.

- Establish that the student must have one petal on the flower in order to get a simple reinforcement, such as a sticker.

- If the student does not follow the expectation, a petal is not given to him/her.

- If the student does not have a petal after the activity period, then he/she does not receive a reinforcement for that activity.

- The student must receive three stickers – or simple reinforcements by the end of the day in order to receive a positive reinforcement, such as a candy bar, at home after school.

- If the student does not meet the criteria, then the student does not receive reinforcement at home for that day.

Make copies of these pages and cut out the petals along the dotted lines:

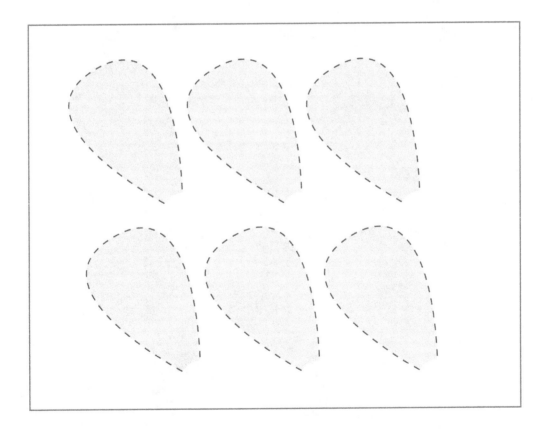

Flower Chart

Name: _____

Social Play Action Figure

Classroom Rights

In this class, I have a right to…

Be treated with respect and compassion.

- ➤ This means no one will treat me unfairly because of my looks, my beliefs, my ideas, or my abilities.
- ➤ This means I have a right to be myself.

Be safe.

- ➤ This means no one will hit me, push me, call me names or hurt me.
- ➤ This means I am able to ask for help and be heard.

Be heard and be able to listen.

- ➤ This means I am able to express myself without being laughed at or interrupted, and to hear others without being disrupted.
- ➤ This means no one will shout, scream, or make disruptive noises when it is time to learn.

Be able to learn to the best of my ability.

- ➤ This means I will not be teased, laughed at or made fun of because of the way I learn.
- ➤ This means I will have access to the materials and the supports I need to help me learn.

I agree to these rights.

Semantic Feature Analysis

Literacy
Semantic Feature Analysis

Brainstorming Maps

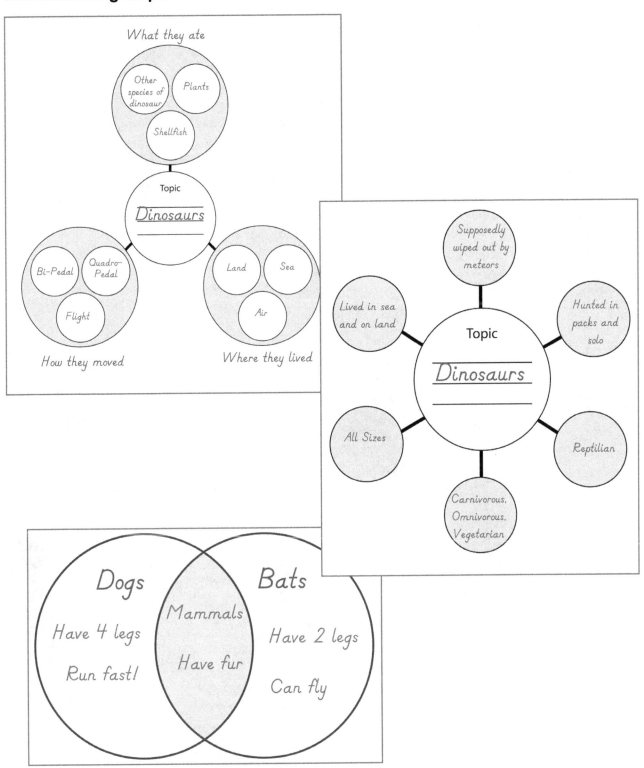

Brainstorming Clusters

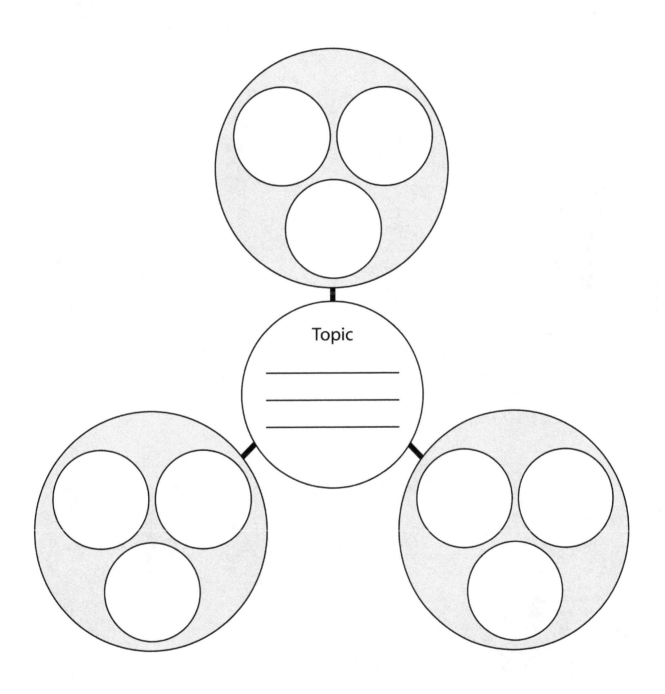

Topic

Brainstorming Array

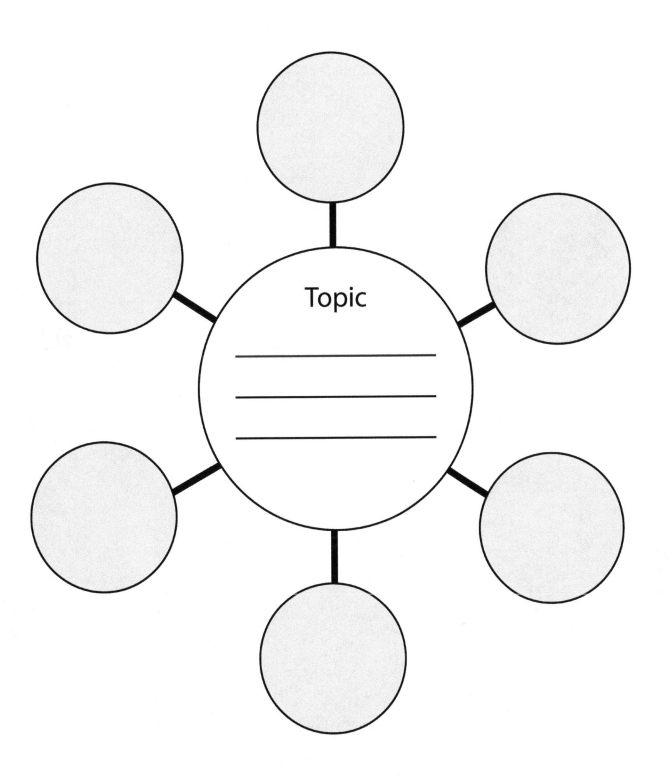

Topic

Circle Diagram

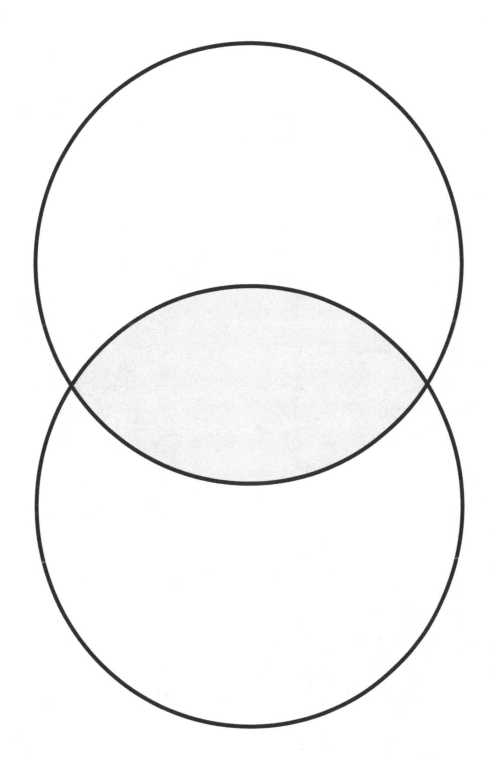

Organizing Maps

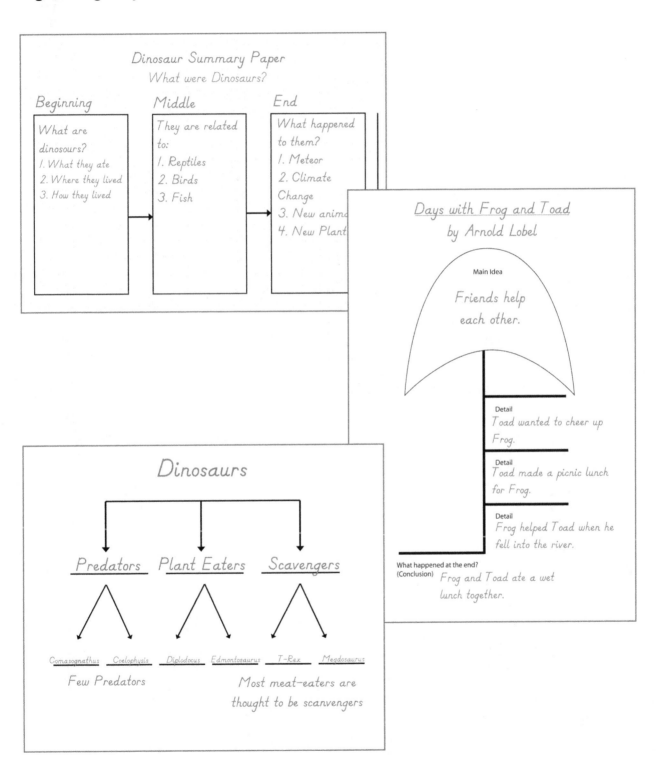

Dinosaur Summary Paper
What were Dinosaurs?

Beginning

What are dinosours?
1. What they ate
2. Where they lived
3. How they lived

Middle

They are related to:
1. Reptiles
2. Birds
3. Fish

End

What happened to them?
1. Meteor
2. Climate Change
3. New anima
4. New Plant

Days with Frog and Toad
by Arnold Lobel

Main Idea

Friends help each other.

Detail
Toad wanted to cheer up Frog.

Detail
Toad made a picnic lunch for Frog.

Detail
Frog helped Toad when he fell into the river.

What happened at the end?
(Conclusion) Frog and Toad ate a wet lunch together.

Dinosaurs

Predators   Plant Eaters   Scavengers

Comasognathus Coelophysis   Diplodocus Edmontosaurus   T-Rex   Megdosaurus

Few Predators

Most meat-eaters are thought to be scanvengers

Boxes & Sequencing

Umbrella Map

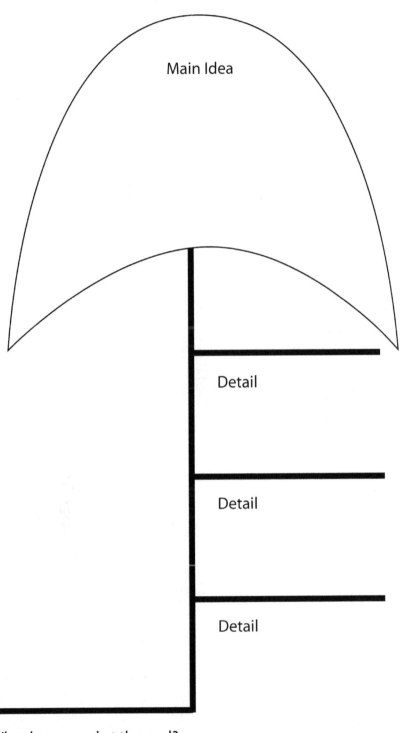

Main Idea

Detail

Detail

Detail

What happened at the end?
(Conclusion)

Tree Map

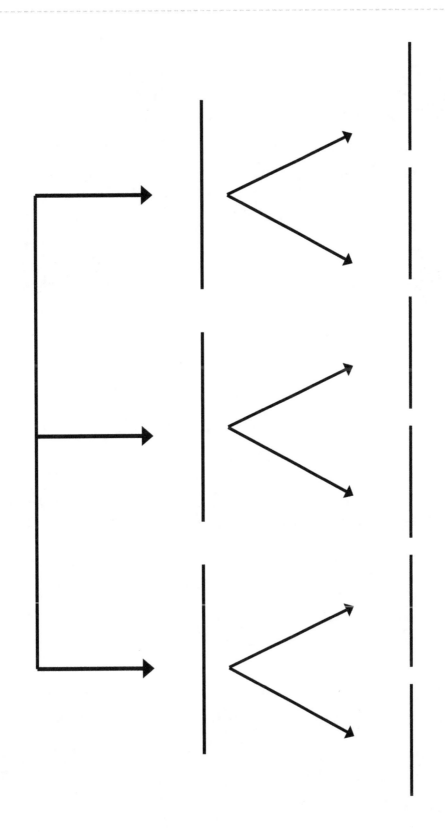

Processing Maps

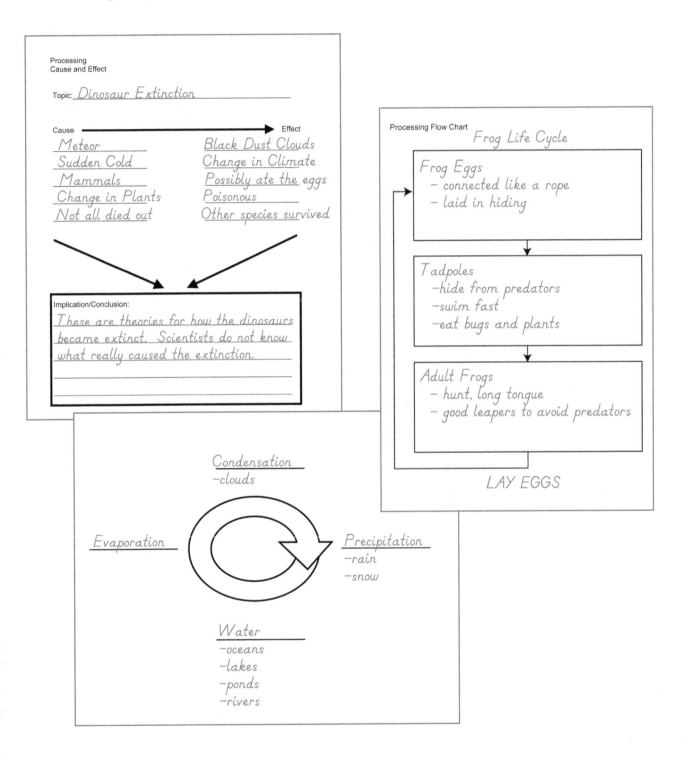

Processing
Cause and Effect

Topic: *Dinosaur Extinction*

Cause ⟶ Effect

Cause	Effect
Meteor	*Black Dust Clouds*
Sudden Cold	*Change in Climate*
Mammals	*Possibly ate the eggs*
Change in Plants	*Poisonous*
Not all died out	*Other species survived*

Implication/Conclusion:

These are theories for how the dinosaurs became extinct. Scientists do not know what really caused the extinction.

Processing Flow Chart

Frog Life Cycle

Frog Eggs
– connected like a rope
– laid in hiding

Tadpoles
–hide from predators
–swim fast
–eat bugs and plants

Adult Frogs
– hunt, long tongue
– good leapers to avoid predators

LAY EGGS

Condensation
–clouds

Evaporation

Precipitation
–rain
–snow

Water
–oceans
–lakes
–ponds
–rivers

Cause & Effect Chart

Topic:_____

Cause ————————————————————▶ Effect

_____   _____

_____   _____

_____   _____

_____   _____

Implication/Conclusion:

_____

_____

_____

_____

_____

Flow Chart

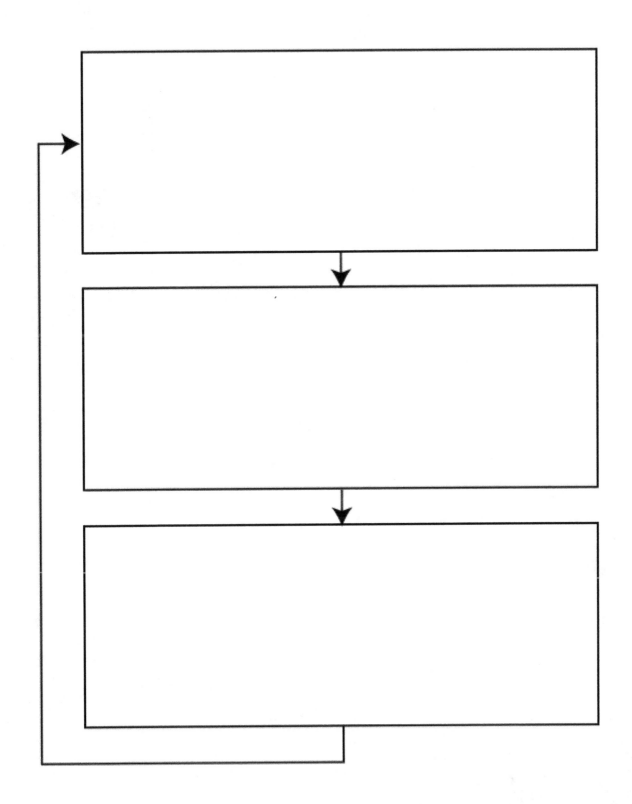

Feedback Loop

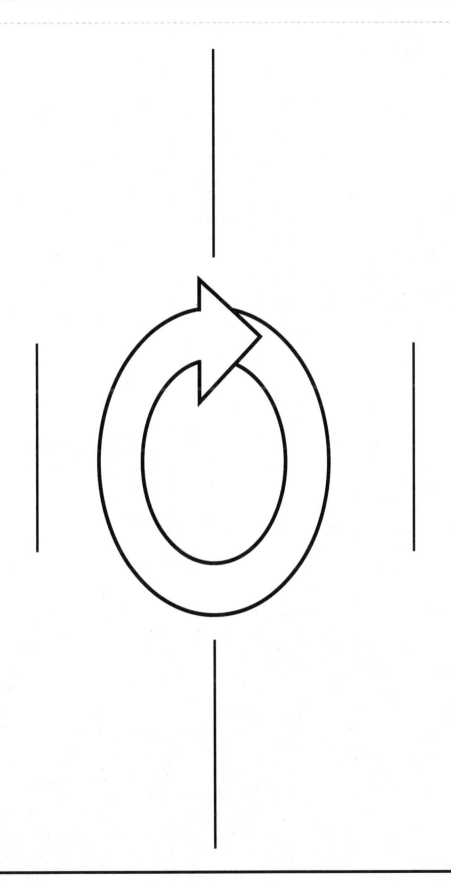

Reading Forms

Title of the Book: Days with Frog and Toad

Author: by Arnold Lobel

The Beginning

Who: Frog and Toad

Where: At the river on an island one afternoon.

When:

What happened first? Toad found a note on Frog's door. It said he wanted to be alone

What happened next?

Toad found Frog at the river.
He was sitting alone.
He was on the island.
Toad said Frog was sad.
He wanted to cheer him up.

Then, what happened?

Toad went home.
He made a picnic lunch to take to Frog.
He went to the island on a turtle.
He fell into the river
The food got wet.

How did the story end?

Frog pulled toad from the river
Toad was sad because the food was wet.
Frog said he was already happy because Toad was his friend.
The two friends sat and ate the food together

When reading, think about:

Who: Frog and Toad

Where: By the river

When: One afternoon

What Happened?

First: Toad found a note on Frog's door. It said he wanted to be alone.

Next: Toad found Frog by the river. Toad said Frog was sad. He wanted to cheer him up.

Then: Toad made a picnic lunch to take to Frog. He fell into the river. The food got wet.

The end: Frog pulled Toad from the River. Frog said he was happy because Toad was his friend. They ate the food together.

Reading Response

Name: C.J.   Date: 2|3|2006

Title of the Book: Days with Frog and Toad

Author: Arnold Lobel

I think the characters in this story were (believable / unbelievable), because...

Frogs and Toads are real, but they don't talk, make picnics, and they can't read.

Reading Organizer

Title of the Book: _____

Author: _____

The Beginning
Who:

Where:

When:

What happened first?

Then, what happened?

What happened next?

How did the story end?

Reading Form

When reading, think about:

Who:

Where:

When:

What Happened?

First:

Next:

Then:

The end:

Reading Response Form

Reading Response

Name:_____ Date :_____

Title of the Book:_____

Author:_____

I think the characters in this story were (believable / unbelievable) because…

_____

_____

_____

_____

_____

_____

_____

Nonfiction Reports

Nonfiction

Title: _Dinosaur Encylopedia_ by Jayne Parsons

Type of Text: (Informational)   Biography

Topic:
Different types of dinosaurs

Description:
Describes the timeline of dinosaurs and the theories about their extinction

Purpose:
Resource of the different dinosaurs and the different geologic eras.

Nonfiction Report

Nonfiction

Title:_____

Type of Text: Informational   Biography

Topic:
_____

_____

_____

Description:
_____

_____

_____

Purpose:
_____

_____

_____

Journal Writing & Story Organizer

Journal Writing

Topic My Day

What are you writing about today? I went horse back riding with my friend Meghan.

What happened first?	Then what happened?
Meghan called and asked if I wanted to go horse back riding with her.	I asked my Mom and she said it would be okay if Meghan's Mom came with us.

Then, what happened?	How did it end?
Meghan's mom picked me up and took us to the barn. She showed us how to brush the horses.	We rode the horses around the corral. If we practace and get better at riding, next time we can go trail riding.

Story Organizer

Title of the Book: Days with Frog and Toad
Author: Arnold Lobel

Characters and Setting:
Who: Frog and Toad

Where: One after noon

When: by the river

What happened first?
Toad found a note on Frog's door. It said he wanted to be alone.

Next...
Toad found Frog at the River. Toad said Frog was sad. He wanted to cheer him up.

And then...
Toad made a picnic lunch to take to Frog. He fell into the River. The food got wet.

How did the story end?

Frog pulled Toad from the river. Frog said he was happy because Toad was his friend. The friends ate the wet food together.

Journal Writing

Journal Writing

Topic _____

What are you writing about today?

What happened first?	Then what happened?

Then, what happened?	How did it end?

Story Organizer

Story Organizer

Title of the Book:_____
Author:_____

Characters and Setting:
Who:_____

Where:_____

When:_____

What happened first?

Next…

And then…

How did the story end?

_____

_____

_____

_____

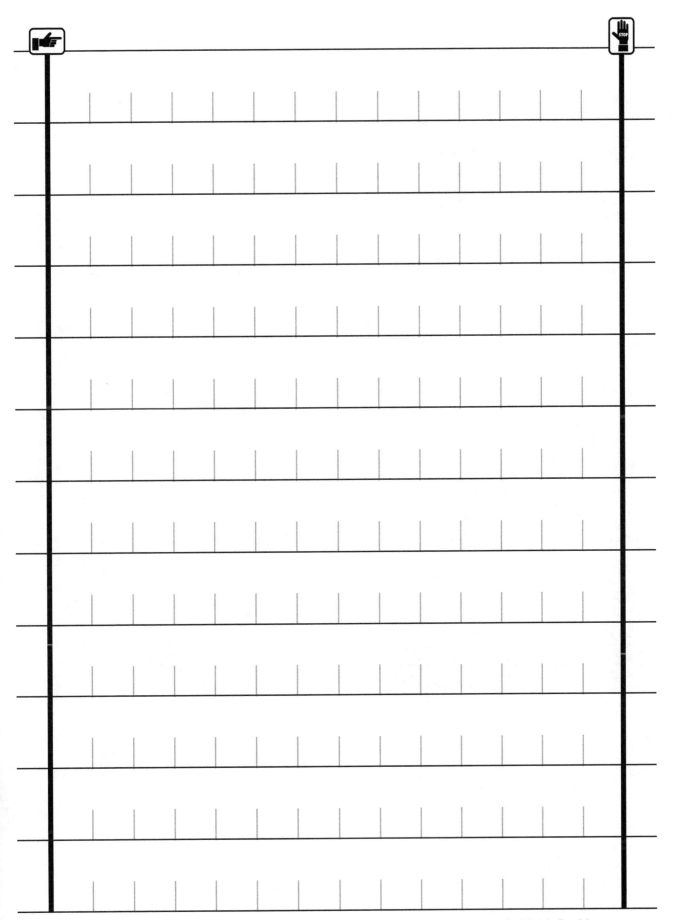

Hundreds Chart

1	2	3	4	5	6	7	8	9	10
11	12	13	14	15	16	17	18	19	20
21	22	23	24	25	26	27	28	29	30
31	32	33	34	35	36	37	38	39	40
41	42	43	44	45	46	47	48	49	50
51	52	53	54	55	56	57	58	59	60
61	62	63	64	65	66	67	68	69	70
71	72	73	74	75	76	77	78	79	80
81	82	83	84	85	86	87	88	89	90
91	92	93	94	95	96	97	98	99	100

Multiplication Table

	1	2	3	4	5	6	7	8	9	10
1	1	2	3	4	5	6	7	8	9	10
2	2	4	6	8	10	12	14	16	18	20
3	3	6	9	12	15	18	21	24	27	30
4	4	8	12	16	20	24	28	32	36	40
5	5	10	15	20	25	30	35	40	45	50
6	6	12	18	24	30	36	42	48	54	60
7	7	14	21	28	35	42	49	56	63	70
8	8	16	24	32	40	48	56	64	72	80
9	9	18	27	36	45	54	63	72	81	90
10	10	20	30	40	50	60	70	80	90	100

CPSIA information can be obtained
at www.ICGtesting.com
Printed in the USA
BVHW052319050720
582964BV00009B/624